APPRECIATIVE INQUIRY

*To my family (Alex, Chloe, and Davy) and friends
(the Older People's Research Group), whose ideas, support,
and contributions are very much appreciated*

APPRECIATIVE INQUIRY

Research for Change

Jan Reed
Northumbria University

SAGE Publications
Thousand Oaks ▪ London ▪ New Delhi

For information:

Sage Publications, Inc.
2455 Teller Road
Thousand Oaks, California 91320
E-mail: order@sagepub.com

Sage Publications Ltd.
1 Oliver's Yard
55 City Road
London EC1Y 1SP
United Kingdom

Sage Publications India Pvt. Ltd.
B-42, Panchsheel Enclave
Post Box 4109
New Delhi 110 017 India

Printed in the United States of America

Library of Congress Cataloging-in-Publication Data

Reed, Jan.
Appreciative inquiry : research for change / Jan Reed.
        p. cm.
Includes bibliographical references and index.
ISBN 1-4129-2746-3 or 978-1-4129-2746-8 (cloth)
ISBN 1-4129-2747-1 or 978-1-4129-2747-5 (pbk.)
    1. Organizational change. I. Title.
HD58.8.R3798 2007
302.3′5—dc22

                                                     2006019604

This book is printed on acid-free paper.

06   07   08   09   10   11   9   8   7   6   5   4   3   2   1

Acquisitions Editor:	Lisa Cuevas Shaw
Editorial Assistant:	Karen Greene
Production Editor:	Denise Santoyo
Copy Editor:	Carla Freeman
Typesetter:	C&M Digitals (P) Ltd.
Indexer:	Pam Van Huss
Cover Designer:	Candice Harman

Contents

Foreword

The tradition of viewing research and intervention (e.g., consultation) as separate processes, yielding wholly different sorts of information, has deep roots in academic and professional cultures. What _counts_ as research is generally considered an important question, and it is important not only for the knowledge that research generates but also for researchers' career paths. "Significant research" is associated with the scientific method, which connotes controlled conditions, objectivity, and pure investigation. The idea that we might, in fact, participate in social transformation by the very process of researching has long been dismissed as research that does not meet the standards of objective science.

Yet we live in a time of rapid social transformation. There are constant demands on us to make pragmatic decisions on the spot, with little time to reflect or inquire. These conditions raise questions about the resources upon which we draw in our decision making. Generally, we would like to believe that sound research informs our decisions. But often it is the pragmatic constraints and possibilities of the situated moment that guide our next move and our long-term planning. The tension between these daily professional demands and the tradition of research that is culturally valued has been a lively (and sometimes heated) topic for the past few decades. Those who have committed themselves to issues of social change have questioned the utility of taking a neutral stance toward research, which, ironically, requires working strenuously to detach themselves from the topics about which they are most passionate.

This tension has been met by great debate among researchers, particularly researchers of social interaction or those who can be identified as "social scientists" (psychologists, sociologists, health care professionals, economists, political scientists, and others). The most common debate is focused on the qualitative/quantitative distinction in research. Another is the distinction between basic research (that which is oriented to generating new knowledge) and applied research (that which will help people be more effective in their worlds). Within these debates, there is recognition that quantitative and basic research are more valued. They generate *new knowledge,* while the outcome of qualitative and applied research requires some situated grounding and therefore is only useful to the very local circumstances of the actual research site.

This volume forges a path toward dissolving these long-standing tensions. The traditional debates are brought into dialogue with each other. Rather than critique the tradition of scientific research—a familiar strategy employed to build a case for alternative research models and methods—Jan Reed, herself a well-trained researcher, eloquently illustrates the ways in which Appreciative Inquiry (AI), a form of practice developed for consultation, can address the criteria expected of research. In the field of consultation, intervention and social transformation are expected outcomes. In research, understanding "what the situation entails" is centered. Yet many have argued that research is a form of social intervention and, in line with this view, Reed addresses how AI can transform and add to traditional research expectations. This volume does not attempt to make a case for AI as the only or best mode of research. Instead, Reed carefully shows how research, particularly in fields focused on social relationships and human interaction, can be both a means for generating new knowledge and understanding while transforming entire communities, organizations, and individuals.

AI is a form of "social construction in action." Within a constructionist orientation, emphasis is placed on *language practices.* This means that knowledge, what we "discover" as researchers, has less to do with any sense of matching observations with "factual evidence" and has more to do with what questions we ask, how we ask them, and who is involved. Constructionists are concerned with the notion of unexamined "factual evidence." Without knowing *who* is determining what counts as a fact and what counts as evidence, and which community's beliefs are being privileged and which community's beliefs are being oppressed, it is difficult to interpret the results of any research program.

As one form of constructionism in action, AI proposes that if we ask questions about problems, we create a reality of problems. On the other hand, if we ask questions about what works or what gives life to a community, group, or person, we participate in the construction of a reality of potential. Frequently misunderstood, this constructionist orientation does not imply that the problems or difficulties people might experience are "not real." They are, in fact, *very* real insofar as we participate in forms of life that are centered on a problem orientation. The point that constructionists address, and that AI in particular illustrates, is that we have *choices* to make concerning what questions we ask, who we ask them of, and how we engage others.

This volume makes three major contributions. First, it introduces AI *in context*. As Reed notes, AI has become a popular consulting tool for organizational development (OD). Many who gravitate toward AI understand the philosophical significance and the theoretical grounding of constructionism as they engage the complex relationship between problem-solving conversations and appreciative conversations. However, for those who do not, AI has become a tool, and often it is a tool that can oppressively prohibit any talk of difficulties or problems. One has to ask, do we really want to deny any and all talk of problems? Can't there be ways to talk about our difficulties that also give rise to an appreciation of how they challenge us toward generative transformation? AI as *one* form of social construction in action, sensitizes the researcher to the language practices of clients, "subjects," and participants. This must include a form of "generous listening," which does not prohibit problem talk, but frames questions that help move problem talk toward appreciation and possibilities within which new ways of coordinating action can be crafted. Reed carefully exposes AI as much more than "happy talk." Her introduction to AI in Chapter 2 identifies the significant shifts in the field of OD and how those shifts have influenced the way we think about processes of change and issues of leadership, for example. A push toward collaborative forms of action, whole-system integration, and a focus on the future provide, as Reed points out, a context where the tradition of problem solving can be augmented with conversation about potential and possibility. By locating AI philosophically and theoretically (Chapter 3), this book underscores that AI is a form of action: a way of engaging with others and thereby creating with those others applicable forms of practice. It is not simply a technique.

The second major contribution of this volume is Reed's ability to address traditional (and nontraditional) critiques and challenges to AI as a research method. Reed's own expertise as a researcher is clear, and her ability to take the questions seriously that arise when one tailors AI to the research context is elegant. The volume begins with a story of her journey through a research project where AI was used. She shares with us her inner dialogue, contemplating the questions she confronted in "justifying" AI as research and not consultation. She also shares the questions and challenges with which she and her colleagues were confronted. In moving through this process with her, the reader fully grasps the serious attention Reed has given the "standard" concerns of the research community and of those investing in a research process. Rather than dismiss the issues raised when comparing AI to a traditional research model, Reed uses these issues as opportunities to carefully consider what we are doing when we participate in any form of research. Research is a transformative process, and, at the same time, research does provide us with "new" knowledge and information. The two goals can comfortably join. At the same time, Reed is very clear in articulating that she is not proposing that AI is better than traditional research or that it should replace more standard modes of inquiry. She engages in thoughtful dialogue about these significant issues.

Finally, this volume offers enormously practical guides for researchers. In Chapter 4, we are introduced to the central issues in AI research: inclusiveness, focus on the positive, sensitivity to sequencing, the researcher's position, and issues of power and control. These issues are extended in later chapters. The discussion of working with communities and various stakeholders to develop research questions (Chapter 5) is particularly inspiring in that it orients a researcher's approach to what is often seen as a very isolated, individual activity. Reed argues,

> One way of thinking about [the development of research questions] is to move away from the idea of research as an individual and private activity, where it is seen as a demonstration of the unique brilliance of the single researcher or team, toward an idea of the research as being a collective activity, where people share and develop ideas together.

As we see, when the broader community of stakeholders is part of constructing the research itself, many common barriers to executing a research project (and/or to gaining funding and other forms of necessary support) are dissolved. This volume does an excellent job of showing how collaboration can productively enhance our research endeavors.

For those struggling to maintain an image of themselves as researchers while venturing out into a more collaborative, nonhierarchical mode of practice, Reed offers reflective activities, case illustrations, and useful resources. We are carried through a research process from conceptualization to interpretation. The message offered in this volume is liberating: Research can be a process of collaborative meaning making through which social transformation is realized (literally, made real) and new ways of knowing are crafted.

—Sheila McNamee

1

Experiences of AI

❖ ❖ ❖

This book, and this chapter, begins with a story: an account of my first experiences of Appreciative Inquiry (AI). This is not because it was a particularly unique experience, but because I hope that it will provide a context and background to this book. I was a researcher who had worked, like many, within a fairly traditional research framework. I came from a health care background, specifically the profession of nursing, and here there was a strong and dominant tradition of experimental research developed in the medical tradition, which contrasted sharply with less structured and more naturalistic methodologies and also had more status with academic and lay audiences. This traditional approach seemed to work well for assessing the impact of medical treatments, but it seemed to work less well when exploring complex and multifaceted phenomena that could not be reduced to well-defined variables or manipulated to fit in with research designs. Through using qualitative approaches, conversations with research participants (or "subjects," as they were called in traditional research) had opened up a world of experiences and viewpoints that made the academic position, in comparison, seem dry and disconnected from the lived world. Engaging with participants, then, was something that I and my colleagues wanted to do, but we were unsure about how to do this and maintain academic credibility at the same time.

Luckily for us, at this point of impasse, we were introduced to Appreciative Inquiry, or AI, and felt that this offered a way of developing collaborative research that would make a useful contribution to debates and developments. As we developed more understanding, however, we started to realize that more work needed to be done if AI were to make a significant contribution to research methodology. AI is an approach that was first developed in the course of reading and using research carried out along relatively traditional academic lines, and it has since gone on to be used as an organizational development (OD) tool. While this has been useful, the links to research development have perhaps been less debated, and so conversations about AI in the research community can be difficult, taking place without shared understanding of goals, principles, and methods. It is with the aim of exploring (or reexploring) the links between AI and research debates that this book has been written, starting off with an account of my first experiences of AI and then going on to tease out ways in which AI connects with research and its traditions. As such, this book is not intended as a definitive text, but, I hope, will serve to raise debates and questions that need to be thought through if AI is to be used to its full potential in research.

❖ WHAT IS AI?

AI is a simple but radical approach to understanding the social world. Put simply, AI concentrates on exploring ideas that people have about what is valuable in what they do and then tries to work out ways in which this can be built on—the emphasis is firmly on appreciating the activities and responses of people, rather than concentrating on their problems. There is, of course, more to it than that, and at different places in this book, a range of ideas will be discussed, but the basic principle of AI is as straightforward as this. The radical aspect of AI is in the way that it challenges us to rethink our ideas on how people work, how change happens, and how research can contribute to this process.

❖ THE WHOLE-SYSTEM EVENT

My first contact with AI came at a point in a research program when the whole team felt uncertain about the way to go forward with a study with many different partners and perspectives. I had been working on a "Whole-System Event" managed by a team from the King's Fund in London, in which 200 people from different professions, agencies, and interest groups had looked at how we could work toward making going home from the hospital a better experience for older people and their families and friends. _Whole-systems working_ explicitly acknowledges the importance of different stakeholders from different groups or agencies in shaping the way things are done, and it seeks to include them in any process of discovery and change. This topic had been suggested at a previous workshop, in which a woman in her 70s (Stella Swinburne) had told us about her experiences when her husband had left the hospital. Her moving story included tales of nurses who had refused to lend her a wheelchair to take her husband to the car and of their arrival back at home on the weekend when no community staff were available to help her and her husband. This story presented a number of difficulties and failures, which galvanized our desire to "solve" these problems. Her audience had decided to meet to try to make this situation better, so that no one else should suffer in that way again, and this led to the Whole-System Event, which was held with participants from a range of service providers and users, including some researchers from local universities.

As part of this work, the whole group had carried out an exercise in which we had divided ourselves into smaller groups according to our roles and remits and sent requests to each other. While the other groups were busy asking each other for help and information, the group that I was with, the researchers, sat at our table in glum silence. Nobody seemed to want to talk to us, and we couldn't think of any messages to send. We had spent so much energy in crafting a disinterested and disengaged stance that we seemed unable to take part in the enthusiastic and animated conversations around us.

Eventually, a message came to us, and it was a request for information: "What research had been done about older people going home from the hospital?" In exploring this question in the discussion that followed, we realized that the other participants in the workshop felt that there would be some research around which to base clear guidelines about what to do and that we would be able to find this research and decipher it for them. As researchers, we had a mixed response to this idea. We felt proud that our academic abilities were recognized and deferred to, and we felt that finding and summarizing the research would be easy. When we started to think about the next stage, in which we were expected to synthesize the research material to provide guidelines for practice, however, we were less confident. We felt not only that the research available would not directly deal with practice but also that we probably didn't have the ability to make that bridge. While we could evaluate each study in terms of its research merit, the conclusions we would reach would be about the way that knowledge had been taken forward and that this knowledge would have academic rather than practical applications.

Looking at Existing Studies

And that is the way it happened. Enthusiastically, we offered to review the research and present it to the group, and we met to plan this event after we had had time to search for available material. When we met, we faced a major problem. We had not been able to find material that related directly to the requests of our colleagues. They wanted to know what the best ways were of managing the processes of older people going home from the hospital. As it was, in an era of guidelines and protocols in U.K. health care, they would ideally have wanted a neat and tidy set of instructions that they could follow. After even a quick look at what we had found (using literature search methods endorsed by librarians), we could see that it would be very difficult, if not impossible, to translate the findings of the studies we had found into clear frameworks for practice. The research we had found was very focused around the incidence of problems and failures, defined in simplistic and decontextualized ways. This meant that it was difficult to draw any lessons for supporting older people through the process of going home and difficult to identify any discussion of the context in which these "discharges" happened. We could not find out much about the organizations and agencies involved, what they had done, or what learning they could offer to others.

When we presented this material to our colleagues, their disappointment was very evident. They could not believe that this research, which seemed costly in terms of time and money, had produced so little of use to them. At the conclusion of the presentation, we all agreed that a different sort of research was needed that would explore different questions and concentrate on practical use rather than esoteric debates about academic rigor. In our conversations, we also became aware of the many innovations and creative approaches that our colleagues were aware of or were using, approaches that were missing from the literature we had found. All of our colleagues were enthusiastic about being involved in a research project, as they had been in the first workshop. We finished by agreeing that we should get together to carry out a study that would be inclusive of all the groups and agencies involved in going home from the hospital, would have clear relevance to practice in a range of different settings, and would respect the developments that had already taken place among the group, which was committed to making things better for everyone involved in going home from the hospital.

First AI Workshops

There we left it, having very little idea about how we could achieve this ambition. We thought about different research models, such as surveys of practice (too unfocused), action research (too focused on problems), and experiments (too difficult to control across such a diverse range of settings). Feeling stuck, we gave up until one of us (Barbara Douglas) came across AI as a way of thinking about community development. She invited us to come to a workshop run by an AI consultant, Anne Radford (http://www.aradford.co.uk). We turned up for this workshop, a range of service users, community workers, agency representatives, and researchers, all of us unsure about what it was about.

In the workshop, we explored the basic principles of AI, starting off with the core principle, that one way to understand the world is to ask questions about achievements, the things that people feel went well, and then to find out what people think helped these things to go well. From this foundation, plans can be developed for taking these ideas forward. This simple premise, however, can be complex to base a study on, and so the workshop then went on to explore ways in which AI could shape exploration and discovery, a process that involved exercises about the ways in which such a study could be carried out, exploring research and OD questions, interview techniques, and processes of analysis.

❖ THE "GOING HOME FROM HOSPITAL" STUDY

Starting an AI Study

The workshop changed the way many of us thought about research. We critically reviewed assumptions that we had about reliability and validity and the importance of distance and noninvolvement as a way of guaranteeing high-quality research. We explored different sorts of research questions and different sorts of research methods, and we set off, optimistically, to conduct an AI study. While we had started off thinking about discharge as being a problem that needed a solution, we started to think about a different focus: People were doing things that worked well. Maybe we could explore these aspects and think about ways of building on them. The core research team that formed to do this was made up of the person whose story had begun the project (Stella Swinburne), two voluntary sector workers from agencies working with older people (Barbara Douglas and Helen Wilding), and two university-based researchers from traditional academic departments (Pauline Pearson and Jan Reed). The larger research group numbered about 40 people who were service users and providers and had become involved through the Whole-System Event or, subsequently, by word-of-mouth.

Perhaps not surprisingly, we hit difficulties. Most of these were about the apparent conflicts that we saw between the "rules" of research and the way that AI was carried out (this was a particular issue for the traditional researchers in the group). Some of these apparent conflicts could be relegated to the category of "unimportant issues" that we would resolve at some point in the future, technical issues about tools and processes; but our discomfort increased when we talked to other researchers about what we were doing. Their reactions ranged from intrigued to aghast, worrying about the seemingly chaotic progress of the study, with decisions being made about who to talk to and what to ask them as the study progressed rather than being carefully planned in advance, as with other, more traditional studies.

This lack of anticipation and planning was in contrast to usual ways of doing research, in which the choices to be made would be rehearsed in advance, as proposals were presented to funders and partners. We were not intending to apply for funding, seeing the work as part of our usual duties, so we had not had to "design" the study in any formal way, although we were limited by the resource and time constraints that our "usual duties" entailed. This allowed us to be creative and organic in the way that we developed the study, but the downside of this was that we made decisions as we went along and did not always have the opportunity to reflect on them or record the thinking behind them. Sometimes, we would be faced with questions about the rationale for our work that we could not answer without great difficulty, as we tried to remember what ideas had guided what we had done.

It became apparent to us that these questions were not just a matter of recording our rationale but also concerned our ideas. The two things were related, of course: Because the ideas were often covert and undeveloped, we sometimes did not even notice that we were having them, never mind how we could keep track of them. What was an exciting and creative process, then, also had elements of doubt and confusion.

Aims, or "What Is the Study Trying to Do?"

Doubt occurred at various points in the study, the process of reflection made much easier by the benefits of hindsight. Perhaps the first point was when we started to think about the aims of the study, in other words, what we might be trying to do with the research. We had started off with a broad and general idea that we should try to find a useful way to "solve" the problems of moving from the hospital to home, and this had changed to an interest in exploring strategies that people had come across and found to be effective under the general principles of AI.

The focus on successful strategies, however, raised many issues, mainly of comprehensiveness and bias. There were concerns that by focusing on positive strategies, we would be painting a picture of practice that would hide problems and difficulties and might make the process of moving from the hospital to home seem an easy business. It might be more useful to seek out a range of stories, rather than focus on what people had felt had gone well. This was a pragmatic point, but another issue was raised by the notion of *bias* as it is used in relation to research, to mean a tendency to be selective in what gets studied and reported. By asking about what went well, we were biasing the study toward success stories and away from negative ones. If research were to present an objective account of what happened, our picture would be skewed toward achievement rather than failure. By these criteria, it would not, by some, be called research at all.

This returned us to the basic principles of AI as we had discovered them in the workshop we had attended. One idea behind AI, we had found, was that exploring what had worked could be a more helpful way of thinking about an issue than examining ways in which things had gone wrong. According to this principle, then, we would achieve more by collecting data about strategies that had worked, or were "successful," so that they could be analyzed and presented to audiences who might want to try them out. This would require us to collect and present sufficient contextual information to enable people to identify similarities and differences with their situations, but in this way, we could make a contribution to the development of practice.

This raised another issue, however, and that was the definition of *successful* that could be used. In our discussions, we had already seen that what was a success for some could be seen as a problem by others, or in other ways. Speeding up the process of going home, for example, could meet the goals of hospital units but create pressure in other parts of the system, such as community services. If this led to problems in delivering services to older people when they got home, the ultimate effect could be to reduce the quality of their experience. While, in traditional research studies, it would be usual practice to define elements like *successful* in precise and perhaps measurable ways, our definitions would have to be open-ended and flexible and, crucially, appreciative: We could not carry out the study based on the idea that some definitions of success were more worthy than others—we had to appreciate them all. We found, then, that what could be thought of as the most unproblematic ideas in a study, in other words, the outcomes it was planned to support, were elusive and diverse and that to carry out a study that would be responsive, inclusive, and appreciative would mean that we had to resist the temptation to develop narrow definitions.

Sampling, or "Who to Involve?"

This variability of possible definitions of success shaped the decisions we made about whom to invite to be involved in the study. As different people in different positions in the discharge process had different ideas of what a successful process would look like, it seemed like a good idea to collect data about and from as many different people as possible, in order to build up an extensive picture of going home from the hospital. This interest in inclusivity was very different from sampling processes that we had come across in other studies. Here, criteria would be drawn up, and a sampling frame would be developed, perhaps with different groupings or stratas and perhaps with target numbers for each strata. For us, in this study, the key factor was whether people had had experiences that they were willing to share with us. We could not know this until we asked them to take part in the study, and we could not ask them this until they were identified by group members. As members would identify people on the basis of their contact and knowledge of them and they would be in contact with different people as the study went on, there could be no prior stipulation of whom to include. As the study was owned by all members, a decision about invitations would be shaped by the ideas of everyone, with all of their variability and diversity.

To encourage participation, we were aware that some negotiations would have to be done by the members who were making nominations. This meant that the sample could not be arrived at through any process of randomization, but had to be strategic and shaped by members' contacts and relationships. While methodology texts did mention sampling strategies, such as "snowball" sampling, in which an initial set of participants would subsequently lead to people to invite, the quantitative research literature seemed to frown on this as being second best to sampling in which the probability of inclusion could be calculated. Qualitative research texts were more concerned with relevance and did talk about "theoretical sampling," in which participants were identified as theory needed development. This model of sampling, however, did not seem to fit with all of what we were planning, which had a huge element of serendipity in it. We had to conclude, then, that we would involve anyone who was suggested and who would be willing to take part, and in the presentation of the study to others, we would need to concentrate on description rather than theoretical justification of the sample.

Methods, or "How Should We Ask Questions?"

Similar issues arose when we started to think about methods. Partly because of resource and time constraints, we had decided that using interviews would be a feasible method of data collection. Although AI provided a template for the questions we would want to ask, we were aware that these questions would be asked in different contexts and in different sorts of relationships. Some people would be interviewed by their managers and others by their clients, for example, and these relationships would affect the way the conversations proceeded. With limits on time and resources, and the transience of many members as they left the group and were replaced by other people from their organizations, we could not hope to train people to carry out interviews with absolute consistency (if, indeed, this is ever possible). The thought of using other methods, such as observation, was equally if not more problematic and would be even more diverse in the many different situations the research would involve.

We had resources to run only a few workshops to explore interview questions, and so we focused again on the process of recording the conversations that they would stimulate. Researchers were given a list of questions that we had collectively debated and agreed to ask, and they were asked to write down responses and check them with the person who had been interviewed. This recording would involve some editing and selection, but this would be done in negotiation between the two people involved in the interview, so it would have an element of validation.

Again, this did not match with the concerns that were evident in descriptions of other studies in which the debates and descriptions were about theoretical imperatives that would lead to the content of the data collection (methodological concerns) and technical debates about the tools used to collect data (concerns about methods). None of these sorts of debates covered the areas we were concerned with: how to foster relevance and a degree of consistency in a study with many participants that would be flexible enough to respond to different concerns and contexts.

Analysis, or "What Can We Find in the Data?"

Having collected the data, we then had to develop a way of analyzing the information that would be true to the collaborative and appreciative nature of the study. We chose an approach known as "Nominal Group Technique" (NGT) (Delbecq & Van de Ven, 1971), in which groups read the transcripts and listed the key points or ideas they had identified in them. These were recorded, with duplications removed and similarities clarified, and the final list was then examined to develop shared definitions.

This process seemed to match up with the guiding principles of the study, but we were aware that the technique was originally proposed as a means of collecting data rather than analyzing them, and data analysis is more often carried out by the use of statistical methods chosen prior to data collection or by the reading and reflection of individuals or small numbers of researchers. A process that involved as many people as we had in the research group had to be collective, and yet the process of inclusivity and responsiveness of a range of interpretations raised questions of responsibility for and ownership of the conclusions of the study. While NGT gave us a framework for reflecting diversity and reaching consensus, this process was very different from other analytic frameworks. Furthermore, from the conclusions of this analysis, we then went on to develop action plans for practice, which introduced yet more idiosyncrasies.

We were not faced with insurmountable problems of differences in interpretation, and the NGT process seemed to move us toward a consensus. We were aware, however, that different interpretations could have been irresolvable, and then we would have been faced with dilemmas about how to convey this diversity in a way that was coherent.

Our work was made more straightforward because one of the processes contained within AI seemed to us to be a good choice to shape the data analysis in a way that would generate ideas for change, the development of *provocative propositions.* Cooperrider, Whitney, and Stavros (2003) described a provocative proposition as follows:

provocative
Proposition

[It is] a statement which bridges the best of "what is" and "what might be." It is provocative to the extent that it stretches the realm of the status quo, challenges common assumptions and routines, and helps suggest desired possibilities for the organization and its people. At the same time, it is grounded in what has worked in the past. (p. 148)

Moving from the themes identified through the process of NGT to provocative propositions was not always a clear process, as themes such as "understanding" or "empowerment" were fairly abstract ideas and the group found it difficult at times to imagine what these concepts would look like in practice. Nonetheless, we had started off with the observation that existing research, while interesting, had not always been used in practice and that researchers had often stopped at presenting findings for others to take up and respond to. Because of this observation, we had felt that we should try to do something else and make the implications for practice clear. The recommendation to develop "provocative propositions," then, was a useful way for us to move from the abstract to the practical.

We did not feel comfortable with stopping at provocative propositions, however, as these became both challenging and puzzling as we thought more about them. While we had moved toward practical findings, we felt that we needed to go one step further. For example, we had identified one theme from the data, "understanding," which many of the interviews had discussed as a key part of effective practice, specifically that people needed to understand the process of going home from the hospital, the procedures and people involved, so that they could plan and make decisions. This could be translated into the provocative proposition "Every worker/patient/carer knows exactly what the other workers do," in which *workers* means everyone involved in the process of discharge (Reed, Pearson, Douglas, Swinburne, & Wilding, 2002, p. 41). This seemed, on first examination, to be quite simple, but as we looked at the proposition more closely, it seemed more difficult. How would this happen, and how would you know if it had? We all had had experiences of organizations that would "inform" people by sending a memo about something and then think that the job had been done. Nobody would read the memo, and it would gather dust in in-trays or on notice boards, and if you betrayed the fact that you had not read it, the senders would blame you—after all, the information was available, and it was your fault if you had not read or understood it.

Action plans

We didn't want this to happen, and so we went on to develop "action plans" from the provocative propositions, which would set out how the propositions could be met and what strategies could be used. This was not very detailed or definitive, mainly because the research had involved many different sorts of organizations, with different processes and resources, so we could not do anything but point to general strategies. We also ended up developing action plans that addressed more than one provocative proposition, because there seemed to be common ground between them once we thought through the implications they had for action. From the provocative proposition "Every worker/patient/carer knows exactly what the other workers do," then, we developed an action plan for informing people, using various strategies, that also addressed other propositions, for example, about developing networks across the system and giving service users information about going home from the hospital. It was not possible, however, to do anything other than distribute our ideas, as other pressures and resource constraints took over and we all had to move on to other work. The process of analysis could have gone on to looking at the implementation of the action plans, but time ran out. In this way, we went only in the direction of implementation and did not actually become involved in it.

Managing the Project, or "Establishing Consensus and Understanding Among the Team"

The difficulties of analysis reflected the overall issues facing us in the management of the study. First of all, there was transience in the group as people started commitments, left commitments, lost interest, or were replaced by their organizations. In a group consisting of members from many different settings, in a period of huge social development, these changes were to be expected, but they still took us by surprise, perhaps because we had seen and heard the enthusiasm of our colleagues and assumed they would stay with the project until it came to an end. As we organized workshops and either received apologies or messages that new people would be joining us, we realized that this wouldn't be the case, and so we had to find ways of keeping the project going and at the same time explaining it to participants who might be new to the process. We developed a very quick guide to AI and to the project, which we hoped would keep people informed, but we were aware that the changes in the group meant that people would be coming to the project in different ways and we would be grateful to just achieve a working consensus, never mind unanimity about the goals and methods of the project.

The issue of transience was not particularly special to an AI project, but some accounts of AI we had read had suggested that this usually had some degree of organizational support. If people did move on, therefore, replacements were available and supported. We were obviously in a very different situation, in which members were faced with organizational responses that could be hostile, oblivious, or at least suspicious.

Another related issue, which raised a number of project management issues, was also related to the characteristics of the group: the diversity of the group members who were drawn from service users and service providers. We were therefore working with people who had not usually worked closely together and had very different perspectives and experiences. This meant that the interpersonal dynamics of the group could be difficult to handle, particularly when some host organizations were in open conflict with each other, for example, competing for resources or arguing about practice. At some points in the study, we even had members writing formal letters of complaint to each other. Even if there was not a conflict, there could be a lack of understanding or knowledge, particularly between professionals, who sometimes did not seem to know much about each other. Again, this is not unique to an AI study, but it was different from the accounts we had read in which people had broadly shared a similar background. This did not mean that they had the same goals, but there was a feeling that they knew more about each other than some of our members did. The challenge for us was to manage the process in a way that meant that the project progressed, but an additional need was for this to be done in an appreciative way, valuing everyone for their experience and the contributions they could make. While the members of the group did take this idea as a basis for working together, we would not claim that the process was wholly friendly and harmonious.

Responses to the Study

The difficulties in developing analytical processes were reflected in the responses we got when we tried to disseminate the findings of the study. As the point of the study had been to develop indications of how practice could develop, we were keen to tell people about it so that they too could build on our findings. To help with this, we presented the study in a number of different ways, including a full report, summaries, and guidelines. While many responses were positive, we still had some experiences in which we were met with suspicion, disbelief, or hostility. When we tried to explore these negative responses, we found that a major problem was that people were unconvinced by the methodology we had described. Because it did not fit into any established framework for reporting, our accounts could potentially read like rambling stories of an ad hoc process. Read this way, people could not always see what it was about the study that should give it any more weight than the impressionistic responses of any other group of people brought together to discuss the issue. Furthermore, as some of our conclusions contrasted with some readers' views, this made suspicion even greater. When we had discussed instances of practice in which people had worked productively across agency boundaries, for example, this was not convincing to readers who had had many negative experiences of interagency problems. In some instances, it appeared that our concern with producing concise summaries for busy practitioners and managers worked against the need to give full explanations of the methods we had used. Because AI was unfamiliar to most of us, without such explanation, the methods could be more easily dismissed.

The community workers, Barbara and Helen, knew about the difficulties facing the practitioners and managers we were attempting to include in the dissemination process. One difficulty was the number of multiple agendas they had to respond to. They had targets to meet and objectives to achieve, and these could be set by a number of bodies and organizations. Someone working in a hospital, for example, would have to meet targets on the care being given to patients, which could include catering, cleaning, and the effectiveness of care, and the discharge process, which could include the speed of the process. It is easy to see how, with these different targets, some might be conflicting or complex. If our guidelines simply added to this complexity by raising other issues or even contradicted some targets, it would be difficult for practitioners or managers to adopt them. Even when no formal targets were set, local and national factors that shape practice could not be easily set aside by the findings of a study that appeared to be lacking in rigor. Even if they were accepted, our guidelines might not always be easily implemented in practice: Processes of change could be tortuous and difficult, and the more radical the recommendations, the more difficult they could be to put into operation.

We also had opportunities to disseminate the work in other arenas, notably the scientific world of conferences and peer-reviewed journals, which was familiar to the researchers in the team. This gave us more space to describe the study, and there were some points that we did not have to explain at length, as we did have a shared vocabulary with readers that gave us some "shortcuts" for description. Nonetheless, we found ourselves challenged by other researchers who were concerned about the validity and reliability of what we had done. One journal, for example, returned the comments of a peer reviewer to us, in which concerns were expressed about our exact research questions and how "representative" the sample was. These questions could have been asked of any qualitative study, of course, and our responses were that these issues were thought of differently in qualitative approaches, that research questions could be fluid and changing as the study progressed, and that samples would be chosen on the basis of relevance rather than the capacity to be representative of a population whose characteristics were unknown and changing. We did get one paper published in an academic journal eventually (Reed et al., 2002), but with others, we were unsuccessful and unable to spend the time to meet reviewers' requirements. In presentations at conferences, we also had problems in fitting our accounts into the conference format. If we presented a paper as a methodological discussion, we could share space with very technical or theoretical accounts from other presenters, and if we presented it as a paper about going home from the hospital, we could present alongside other more straightforward papers that dealt with the topic from more well-understood perspectives. Neither of these felt comfortable, raising more questions for us and the audiences than we could explore.

Even so, it seemed that there was a more fundamental conflict between the traditions of "objective" and disinterested science and what we had done, which seemed subjective and partisan. At its basic formulation, this conflict could be phrased as a question: How could we argue that we had discovered something, rather than just seen what we wanted to see? With our optimistic fervor as new converts to AI, perhaps we were simply carried away by the enthusiasm and novelty of the approach?

As a team, we felt discouraged and a little offended by these criticisms. How dare they accuse us of such devious approaches to study? We knew that we had not been "swept away," and indeed one of the team had not been to the original AI workshops and had remained a voice of constructive skepticism throughout. We felt that this was a useful contribution, as it made us explore our reasons for doing what we had done at several points in the study, and that the process of justifying our strategies to someone who remained somewhat distant from the AI debate had been an important one: If we could argue to her satisfaction, we felt confident that we were on firm ground. Even without this, we felt that we had gone through a process of reflection and deliberation that was rigorous and detailed at each point in the study.

While these did not fit into traditional academic research frameworks, they nonetheless seemed robust to us and far removed from the uncritical and evangelical zeal that some academics attributed to organization developers and consultants. As we heard more and more voices expressing disquiet about AI, we also discerned discomfort with what they saw as the genesis of the approach in the field of OD, in which consultants received large fees for advising organizations that would not be able or willing to critique the methods used. The commercial element could be seen to encourage consultants to tell organizations that they were doing well and to elicit success stories, as organizations would be well-disposed toward funding this. Thus, for some, the substantial theoretical thinking of AI was overshadowed by what could seem to be the attention-grabbing publicity of AI consultants.

❖ SUBSEQUENT EXPERIENCES OF AI

Throughout this study and afterward, I have been involved in three main ways of trying to work with AI: first, writing proposals for funding; second, carrying out studies; and third, supervising students. These activities have raised a number of issues, similar to those we had experienced when trying to publish our work, and these seem to be about funders', members', audiences', and examiners' ideas of what "good" research is. While we may have come to reconsider our ideas about the characteristics of good research, this is not necessarily shared or understood by the people with whom we discuss our research. While it is tempting to dismiss these differences and concentrate on developing ideas only with like-minded people, this seems a rather closed and rigid position. As AI is an approach that encourages inclusion and debate, it would be ironic not to explore it by thinking about the different positions that different audiences might have and the points that they might make.

For funders, for example, this idea of "good" research can often be a traditional "scientific" model, in which studies are comprehensive and valid in statistical terms. Funders may be looking for studies that cover a wide population and ask a wide range of questions. An AI proposal, on the other hand, will be focused, and it may be looking at a tightly defined group and asking what might appear to be a narrow range of questions. AI proposals, then, might not look like value for the money to funders. In addition, they might ask for funding for things that funders might not have supported before, such as coresearchers' time and expenses. If funders usually fund researchers employed by the applicant's agency (and prefer to deal with only one named applicant), it may be difficult to persuade them to fund an AI study that has collaboration at its heart.

Experiences of carrying out AI studies have tested this notion of collaboration to the full. As the discussion above of the "Going Home From Hospital" study has indicated, people come to AI studies from different backgrounds and with a range of ideas and expectations, and these may be very different from each other and from AI. These ideas may include a general suspicion of research or a suspicion of anything that does not conform to traditional ideas of research, and the challenge for AI may be to establish its own logic and rationale for members of AI projects and for the audiences they may reach.

Similar considerations affect students using AI, as examiners with traditional ideas of methodology look for assurances that the work is the student's own and that it will demonstrate learning about research. A collaborative study may blur boundaries between the researcher and the coresearchers, to the extent that it is difficult to tell who has done what and therefore who should get the credit for it. Another feature of AI is that research designs can often develop organically, and so it might be difficult for a student to show the type of "knowledgeable planning" that would demonstrate methodological competence.

These experiences have not been entirely negative, and for myself and colleagues, engaging with people with different ideas of research has provided opportunities for learning, as we make connections between different ways of thinking and doing. While we have felt confident about the value of what we are doing, explaining this to others has led us to reexamine some of the assumptions that we have been close to taking for granted, overall a healthy process that has, we feel, led to increased robustness of our AI research. It is this process of reflection and exploration that has led to this book, which seeks to make the links between AI and research activity more visible and open to debate. For readers who are trying to make these connections themselves, I hope that it will be useful and that it can make a contribution toward integrating AI with other approaches in the researcher's repertoire.

❖ AIMS OF THE BOOK

Reflecting on these experiences of using AI, I have been struck by the way we have all been able to stay with the process and the way we feel that it has been worthwhile. At a recent lunch meeting, where some members of the team from the "Going Home From Hospital" study were present, we all remembered how confused we had been at times—but also how we and all the other participants had enjoyed the process and how for some of us, it had changed the way we thought about our work. Other people at the lunch, who had been involved in other AI projects, echoed our feelings. This conversation, with the positive feel that we had about using AI, went some way toward balancing out accounts that we had given of the AI process as difficult and perplexing (an emphasis that this chapter may have moved toward at times).

That we had survived and enjoyed the process of discussing AI with different audiences was a good thing, but it did seem that it would have been useful for us to have had some resource that could have discussed the issues we faced. These were sometimes the same issues that anyone using AI as an OD tool would encounter, but there was also another layer of debate, which had to do with the way AI related to the world of research and what it was to make AI research decisions rather than the choices that other approaches suggested. For me, in particular, my work in a university, with academic traditions, meant that many of the challenging questions that had been posed to me were about the validity of the approach in terms of traditional research methodology, and as I met and discussed AI with other researchers who were using it, it became clear that they had mused over similar questions. Our shared curiosity about AI and the issues that it gave rise to were a starting point for this book.

The aim of the book, then, is to provide a resource for researchers that explores and explains AI in a way that adds to the researcher's toolkit. This is not a mission of conversion—I would not argue that AI is the best or only valid approach to investigation, but rather that it can do some things in some situations and can provide a different perspective on questions that have seemed underexplored despite much previous research in the field. This does not mean that I am trying to provide answers to all the questions that are asked of AI—some of them can be answered in many different ways, and some may have to be left unresolved. While living with gray areas might, in itself, be an achievement that should be appreciated, I hope that in this book, readers will at least come to know what those areas are.

The book is divided into two main sections, the first exploring general principles and debates in AI, particularly the ways in which the growth of AI as a tool for change and development in organizations can and has informed the use of AI as a research methodology. This chapter begins this first section, presenting initial experiences of AI, the questions that it raised, and the ways it offered a new and effective way of doing research. Chapter 2 gives a fuller description of AI, outlining the history and development of AI, from initial ideas to more recent frameworks, including some of the theoretical ideas that have informed this development. Chapter 3 moves from looking at AI as an OD approach to looking at AI as a research approach, by making connections between AI and models of research in the social sciences. A number of connections are made between the ideas that inform AI and schools of methodology, as part of the process of identifying common themes. These abstract discussions are taken forward in Chapter 4, in which the position of the researcher using AI as a research methodology is discussed, particularly the issues of roles and relationships inside and outside of the study.

The second part of the book focuses on the stages of research and the implications of using an AI approach in each stage. Chapter 5 discusses developing research questions and goals, including the aims and expectations of researchers, funders, practitioners, and participants. Chapter 6 discusses the process of managing and organizing data gathering, in which issues of partnership and collaboration are key. Chapter 7 discusses the process of analyzing or making sense of data—the ways stories are told and questions raised. Chapter 8 talks about some of the issues around communicating and disseminating AI research, issues of audience and voice. Chapter 9 brings the book to a close, discussing ideas about the ways AI research can go forward. True to the spirit of AI, this chapter reviews the potential and strengths of AI research and builds on this to outline ways in which it might develop in the future.

The chapters in the second part of the book do follow a loosely chronological structure, in that they each concentrate on stages of research as they can present themselves in sequence: First, research is planned, data are collected, and the collected data are analyzed, and then reports are written and the research disseminated. Finally, as the "peak" of research activity, theories are developed. This chronological sequence, however, is more of a device for organizing the book than a reflection of the way research happens. It can be very difficult to follow a neat and tidy plan, as research responds to changing ideas and circumstances. The chronological structure of the book, then, serves more for the reader to find topics and discussions than a template to follow by researchers.

Reflecting the complexity of research, the book also addresses a range of themes that shape inquiry, themes that are not necessarily unique to different chronological stages of research, but seem to have some affinity with them. Chapter 5 explores ideas about audiences and expectations of research, which can be evident in the stages of planning research, and this discussion uses the idea of communities as a way of thinking about the different potential participants in inquiry. Chapter 6 uses the idea of data collection and its complexity in AI to discuss the idea of partnership and collaboration in AI as groups come together to carry out studies in ways that are inclusive but can also give rise to questions about the nature of their contributions. Chapter 7 focuses on data analysis, but on the issues of story and questioning—again, how different participants may view data differently. This idea of different positions is also taken through to Chapter 8, in which ideas about the diversity of audience, message, and interest are related to the processes of dissemination and communication. In Chapter 9, the motif of change is revisited, drawing on previous chapters to consider the processes of developing ideas, frameworks, and theories, as a way of understanding and facilitating processes of change. Crosscutting and underpinning these foci are themes about inclusivity and a focus on the positive; dimensions of chronology or timeliness of the steps of AI; and the position of participants, a dimension that also involves discussions of power and control. These discussions have been included in Chapter 4, in which the possibilities of bringing together AI principles and those of research are outlined before the more detailed discussions of the following chapters.

The structure of this book, then, incorporates the more orthodox methodological discussions of the stages or steps of research, with some of the key themes and ideas that are integral to any debates about AI. Trying to integrate the concrete and the abstract in this way has been a challenging task, and readers can judge whether and in what ways this integration has been achieved. The reader also needs to think through whether the book amounts to a useful and convincing exposition of AI: The idea is not to develop definitive approaches to AI, but to open it up to debate and discussion and give readers an overview that will be a basis for making up their own minds about whether AI can be a useful approach to creating a research basis for change. Making this decision will involve readers in a process of reflection on ideas of research, both those of others and their own.

2

A Brief Tour of the History and Principles of AI

The previous chapter began this book with a personal account of a "discovery" of Appreciative Inquiry (AI)—an account that resonates with Steier's (1991) argument that all research is ultimately autobiographical, in that researchers are an essential part of a study (p. 5). For myself and my colleagues, this part was played out in the way that we took an approach most commonly used for organizational development (OD) and tried to make sense of it as a research framework. This account is offered, then, in order to provide a context for the debates of these next chapters about how AI can be used as a research methodology. First, however, this chapter gives a brief history of AI and its more well-known growth as an OD tool. This will describe the processes of AI in order to give readers a basic introduction to some of the key ideas and methods that have been developed. The next chapters will focus on AI as a research tool, in other words, how the ideas in this chapter connect to debates about the way research can be carried out. This is not to deny the research roots of AI or to say that it has not been concerned with issues of method, but rather to observe that these concerns take on a different aspect when they are aired in the arena of research methodology.

❖ THE BEGINNINGS OF AI

There are many accounts of the development of AI, and they all tell pretty much the same story. This story is about the experiences of David Cooperrider, who, while doing a PhD study on organizational dynamics (completed in 1986), took an approach that, at the time, was very different from the established methodologies of organizational research. Interviewing a number of doctors in a hospital in the United States, Cooperrider found that asking questions about their work that invited them to describe and discuss the aspects they valued seemed to encourage people to talk in an unrestricted way. When he examined what they had said, it seemed to be very interesting and provided a basis for building on these achievements to come to an understanding of ways in which work could be enhanced and ideas applied—in other words, the findings of the study could contribute to change.

Cooperrider was a doctoral student, and one of the requirements he would be trying to meet was that his study would produce new and unique insights, a traditional criterion for this type and level of work. He seems to have succeeded. People were talking about issues that had not been explored before, that is, what they were proud of. There was a body of research that addressed the stresses and strains of health work and the problems that practitioners faced, but not much discussion of what had gone well and what had helped it to do so. This was new data. Furthermore, the way Cooperrider was able to conduct these conversations and the methods he used to explore achievement were in themselves innovatory. Asking positive questions seemed to be a very productive approach in both finding new information and exploring new methods.

The basic idea of asking questions that were _appreciative_ had been born, but from this beginning, much more work has been done. The methods of AI have been refined and developed by Cooperrider and others as the approach has been adopted across a range of different organizations and contexts. The focus has primarily been on OD; that is, it is centered around processes of change in and across organizations, often with an AI practitioner working as a facilitator or consultant. This focus has led to the discussion and development of experiences and insights of AI in this context.

Watkins and Mohr (2001) have described this process of growth and development in a timeline that stretches from 1980 to the present day (the timeline can also be seen at the Appreciative Inquiry Commons Web site, http://appreciativeinquiry.cwru.edu/intro/timeline). This history includes the details of the first project using the approach, the

Cleveland Clinic Project, which was Cooperrider's (1986) doctoral study, in which the outline of AI was first developed. Cooperrider was given permission by the director of the Cleveland Clinic to focus on the positive factors that people had discussed, and from examining these responses, he began to think through the implications of taking a radical new approach to developing organizations, one that started with building positive ways of working rather than immediately concentrating on identifying problems and devising ways of solving them. This was also supported by some research findings that had been published over the years in a range of different disciplines and traditions but had not been brought together to inform ideas about research and OD (Cooperrider, Whitney, & Stavros, 2003, pp. 10–13). The following is a brief description of this research.

One body of work was the research done on _placebos_, which had *placebos* found that patients who were given "dummy" treatments, which supposedly could not exert an influence on health, seemed to feel better. This placebo effect was frowned upon by those who thought the patients were simply subject to the psychological effects of the placebo, to the extent that treatments and research studies would be used to try to "control" the placebo effect. Another way of thinking about the placebo effect, however, is that it is a demonstration of the power of the mind and that rather than be "controlled," efforts should go toward enhancing and exploring it.

Another set of results was the findings of the "Pygmalion" stud- *Pygmalion* ies in schools. Here, teachers were given information about the abilities of their pupils, that they were very able, averagely able, or *ability-* not very able. These descriptions were randomly assigned to pupils, *focused* regardless of their actual performance, but as time went on, the pupils' test scores began to match up with the statements that their teachers had been given: Pupils and teachers were living up (or down) to these expectations.

Another body of work addressed "learned helplessness." In *learned* response to the suggestion that they were unable to change their situa- *helpless-* tions, it was found that people became apathetic and hopeless. *ness*

Another set of studies indicated that people could imagine their world and their future much as they could visualize an "inner newsreel." If encouraged to do this, they could envision future scenarios and possibilities in detail, and they could also respond to positive imagery in ways that were creative and constructive.

These studies suggested that people could be highly influenced by their expectations and those of others. This research therefore could be interpreted as supporting some of the early AI ideas, for example, that asking positive questions facilitated positive behavior. This justification has, however, been questioned by Patton (2003), who has argued that some of this research has been challenged subsequently, either through questioning the findings or the interpretations of it. This positivity also contrasted with orthodox models of organizations, which, as Hamel (2000) has suggested, are based on the notion of "continuous improvement," in which reviews of changes would assume that there needed to be further initiatives implemented as organizations became complacent. This idea, Hamel argued, has "reached the point of diminishing returns" as the pressure to keep changing organizations, rather than affirming them, runs out of energy. Whitney (1998) pointed out that these development models are *deficit based* (p. 314); that is, they start with the assumption that the organization is a problem needing to be fixed because it is unsatisfactory, inadequate, or underperforming. The AI approach, in contrast, is *strengths based,* in that it begins with understanding and then builds on the strengths of an organization. Whitney also pointed out that many OD strategies are not truly inclusive. They typically involve small groups working on change strategies, with restricted involvement from everyone else in the organization. This also contrasts with the AI insistence on widespread inclusion and involvement across the organization.

At about the same time as the initial Cooperrider study was taking place, Gergen published a seminal work, *Toward Transformation of Social Knowledge,* in 1982, which critiqued existing research traditions and pointed to a new direction in social theory development that built on, rather than sought to control, the interaction between research and practice. This direction also paid attention to the processes of developing ideas as people got together to "co-construct" interpretations that could have a powerful impact on the way they acted. This work fitted in with some of the AI ideas that were beginning to take shape and added some momentum to their generation and refinement, providing a theoretical foundation for taking Cooperrider's work forward.

A series of presentations and discussions of these ideas took place at conferences and meetings, many of these for OD practitioners; also, Cooperrider completed his thesis in 1986. This doctoral work began to be published in a range of different journals and books, and as others became interested in the approach and tried it for themselves, the body of work grew. AI publications varied: There were some accounts of situations in which it had been used in OD, and there were some handbooks, manuals, and textbooks published.

Some writers and consultants had been working along AI lines before this, having independently developed the ideas themselves.

Others had been working along more traditional lines but had felt uncomfortable with them, and AI answered many of their concerns. Others still had been comfortable working with problem-solving models and had only begun to think about other ways of working when they came across AI. Whatever the route, increasing numbers of people began to use AI and to use this language to describe what they did. Making links to the theoretical debates of social constructionist thought, as explored by Gergen, allowed AI practitioners to frame their work in a wider way, connecting with theories about the way the social world is in general, not just about how organizations change.

A number of high-profile development projects also received attention at this time. One of the most famous, because of its scope and impact, was the "Imagine Chicago" project, led by Bliss Brown in 1992. Here, the people of Chicago interviewed each other to find out what they liked about the city and how they could build on this (see http://www.imaginechicago.org for details and updates). Another high-profile project has included the facilitation of the interreligious faith group convened by the Dalai Lama (see http://www.appreciative inquiry.cwru.edu/ for details), in which leaders of various religious groups have met together to develop a way forward toward religious peace. These projects have been wide-ranging, crossing different groups and organizations, but some have also focused on small agencies or groups.

As the ideas of AI spread, more interest and support groups developed; training workshops were held; and ideas and experiences were shared. Forums were conducted on the World Wide Web, for example, the Taos Institute, set up by Ken and Mary Gergen and others in 1990 (see http://www.taosinstitute.net); the AI Listserv, set up in 1997 by Jack Brittain at the University of Texas (see http://www.aipractitioner .com); the electronic *AI Newsletter*, set up by Anne Radford in London in 1998 (http://www.aradford.co.uk); and journals devoting special issues to AI. One key journal was the *OD Practitioner*, which devoted the millennium special issue to AI, as a key movement toward the future of OD. As interest spread, people began to think of AI not just as a set of techniques for change but also as "a philosophy and orientation to change that can fundamentally reshape the practice of organizational learning, design and development" (Watkins & Mohr, 2001, p. 21). Coghlan, Preskill, and Catsambas (2003) went on to argue that "As such, it is both a philosophy and a worldview, with particular principles and assumptions and a structured set of core processes and practices for engaging people in identifying and co-creating an organization's future" (p. 6).

As the debate widened across the community of AI practitioners, a number of ideas about AI were explored and refined, and these have become important ways of understanding and communicating AI. They are usually described as "principles," the concepts and values on which AI is based; the "assumptions," which flow from these and guide action; and "processes," which are the ways in which the principles and assumptions of AI are put into practice. To get a fuller idea of AI, these elements are described next.

❖ PRINCIPLES

The five principles of AI are discussed in many texts, but they originated in the work of Cooperrider's first descriptions of AI. They follow on from the key ideas from previous research, mentioned above, and the work that Cooperrider had done himself.

The Constructivist Principle. This principle is related to social constructionist theory (Gergen, 1982, 1999) and the idea that our thoughts about the world are developed through interpretation and construction, rather than merely the simple recording of phenomena. This means that as different people interpret the world, there are different stories of what is happening, existing alongside each other, and attempts to establish the "truth" by checking the factual accuracy of accounts ignore these possibilities of interpretation. For AI, attention is paid to the processes of construction, in the way people can come to tell different stories about the past, present, and future and the way these stories have the power to shape and reflect the way people think and act.

The Principle of Simultaneity. This principle points to the way that inquiry and change are simultaneous; in other words, they are not separate and sequential stages in development. An *inquiry* is an intervention in the way it stimulates reflection and thought that lead to different ways of thinking and doing, and this needs to be acknowledged throughout AI work.

The Poetic Principle. This principle emphasizes the way that people author their world continually, choosing the parts of their stories they are most interested in at the time and experimenting with different "plotlines." AI needs to support people through this individual and collective process, engaging their attention and energy and taking them through the authoring process in a way that makes it accessible to them.

The Anticipatory Principle. This principle suggests that the way people think about the future will shape the way they move toward the future. If, for example, they see the future as full of possibility, they will move toward these possibilities. Conversely, if they feel that the future is bleak and hopeless, they will feel that there is no point in doing anything that will only be a waste of energy. In AI, starting off with an idea of the future that is based on what works well directs energy toward exploring ways in which this can be developed further.

The Positive Principle. This principle suggests that a focus on asking positive questions (as in AI) engages people more deeply, and for a longer time. This, it is argued, is because people naturally turn toward ideas and images that provide nourishment and energy. Capturing people's interest, therefore, is an effective way of getting them involved in change, and the way to capture interest is most effectively done by inviting them to explore positive questions. AI incorporates the positive principle in the way it asks questions.

These five principles make the links between theoretical developments across a range of disciplines, for example, human development, interaction, organizational and learning theories, and the starting points for AI. These five principles are important, but they are also quite abstract, and so the development of AI assumptions, essentially the principles translated into the statements that AI work can begin with, help to clarify the process of doing AI.

❖ ASSUMPTIONS

In every society, organization, or group, something works. This is sometimes a difficult point to make when participants are gloomy or despondent, feeling that they are part of a group in which nothing works. Exploring this assumption may mean that the facilitator needs to go back to basics. For example, the fact that people are sitting together in a room to embark on AI work suggests that there is something about the communication system, the housekeeping system, or the building maintenance that has worked to bring people together: The phone calls or memos worked, room booking worked, and the room has electricity, walls, a roof, and doors. People might not have had much information about the day, the room might not be big enough, and the equipment might be unreliable, but essentially, the basics worked.

What we focus on becomes our reality. In choosing to focus on what works, participants create a sense of possibility rather than a sense of limitation. By drawing attention to what people feel has been achieved, the reality they experience is one in which things can be done well, whereas focusing on problems creates a reality in which things are always failing.

Reality is created in the moment, and there are multiple realities. This assumption builds on the poetic principle, of drawing attention to the way AI can move to exploring the story-authoring process and work with multiple realities, rather than spending time searching for a single "truthful" account in which the facts can be checked and verified.

The act of asking questions of an organization or group influences the group in some way. This assumption links with some of the work on change theory and the principle of simultaneity, which suggests that asking questions gets people to think about their activities in new ways and that this thinking can lead to new ways of doing.

People have more confidence and comfort to journey to the future (the unknown) when they carry forward parts of the past (the known). This recognizes that, for many people, doing new things is a process that arouses fear and anxiety. Exploring and building on current acts, rather than proposing a start that will begin from a rejection of all that has gone before, gives people the confidence to go forward: It reaffirms their worth, ability, and potential.

If we carry parts of the past forward, they should be what is best about the past. This follows from the previous assumption but emphasizes the importance of looking at the best of what has been done. This gives direction and shape to AI work, with clear messages for exploration and expansion.

It is important to value differences. This assumption reflects the importance of different views and perspectives, which need to be appreciated. The temptation to work toward a consensus and in the process ignore differences comes from ideas about the aims of the work found in traditional models of OD, rather than AI.

The language we use creates our reality. Again, this assumption draws on ideas from social constructionist thought, which emphasizes the importance of language in the process of constructing reality (Hammond, 1996).

These statements are called "assumptions" in the literature, which suggests that they go unquestioned and unchallenged by practitioners.

This is not the case. It is more that they are the results of a long process of thought and discussion, starting with research and theory and moving toward practical guidelines. They are presented as the definitive statements that are a result of this process simply because this makes them easier to communicate, but this does not mean that they should be regarded as being beyond question.

❖ STARTING AI WORK

Choosing Topics

One of the first steps in AI is selecting the focus or topic for the *positive core* inquiry, and this should reflect the positive core of an organization. As Cooperrider et al. (2003) argued, the choice of topic "sets the stage" for AI. It begins with discovering the "life-giving story" of the organization and goes on to the development of "bold hunches" about what this is and what people will want to find out more about (p. 32). Cooperrider et al. gave examples of questions that can be asked to help select a topic:

> "What factors give life to this organization when it is and has been most alive, successful, and effective?" (p. 32). This question seeks to discover what the organization has done well in the past and is doing well in the present.

> "What possibilities, expressed or latent, provide opportunities for more vital, successful, and effective (vision-and-values congruent) forms of organization?" (p. 32). This question asks the participants to dream about and design a better future.

Cooperrider et al. (2003) went on to state that "topics can be anything related to organizational effectiveness. . . . They can include technical processes, human dynamics, customer relations, cultural themes, values, external trends, market forces, and so on" (p. 37). With such a wide range of potential topics, AI can be used to explore many dimensions of organizational life, although Cooperrider et al. suggested that this is best restricted to three to five compelling topics, with the following characteristics:

> They are affirmative or stated in the positive.

> They are desirable; that is, they identify the objectives that people want.

They are topics that the group is genuinely curious and wants to learn more about.

They move in the direction that the group wants to go in.

Topics can be determined before AI work begins, when the organization itself identifies a focus or an issue that it wants to tackle. This has the power of relevance to the organization, reflecting the key challenges or questions it faces. The topic does need to be chosen with support across the organization. If it is the concern of only a small group of individuals within the organization (who may have control of the funds to resource the AI work), the topic may need to be affirmed or modified to foster widespread participation across the organization. Similarly, if the preselected topic has been defined in terms of deficits rather than strengths, some preliminary work may need to be done to open up thinking about the positive core of the organization, so that AI work can begin from a basis that is in tune with the spirit of AI. A focus decided by a few people in the organization or one that is built around deficits or problems is not a useful basis for AI work, conflicting with the strengths-based approach to development.

Cooperrider et al. (2003) clearly stated the importance of choosing topics for AI, arguing that "human systems grow in the direction of their deepest and most frequent inquiries" (p. 37). They went on to assert that the process of topic choice is a fateful act, as it shapes the direction of growth. This may be partly because topic choice and formulation are part of a process of changing ideas: By choosing affirmative language, thinking is affected—or, as Cooperrider et al. said, "Words create worlds" (p. 38).

Inviting Participation

Another question is one of participation: Who should be involved in the AI work? This chapter has already noted Whitney's (1998) critique of traditional approaches based on limited participation and discussed the drive in AI to include a wide range of participants. This is useful as a general indication, but when doing AI work, more complex questions can arise. Having established that inclusion should be widespread, there are still choices to be made: first, about who to invite (which parts of the organization, which people, and whether people outside the organization should be involved) and, second, about how this invitation should be made (through existing networks or independently, with full or minimal information).

Cooperrider et al. (2003) argued that "an important criterion in selecting participants is their ability to bring viewpoints and experiences from many different levels of and from many different perspectives about the organization" (p. 35). This points to the need to include as many people as possible, so that they can contribute, but at the beginning of AI work, it may be difficult to identify who these people are. Some key players in an AI development may become clearly known only as the work proceeds. The choice of invited participants may also extend beyond the organization—where customers and users, key partner organizations, and professional or trade associations might be involved. Again, inclusivity is the key, and too narrow a definition of relevance may lose some interesting insights. Sometimes an observation by someone who was not initially thought to be in a central position can make an important difference to the way change happens. The problem is that you won't always know who this person is until you start AI working.

The second question is about how invitations should be made. In some organizations, communications can be hierarchical and coercive—commands rather than requests. This is not in keeping with the spirit of AI and so should be avoided. A group of people brought together through the delivery of an impersonal memo that has given them no choice but to attend are not going to be willing to engage in a process that requires a collaborative spirit of openness and appreciation. One way to dispel the expectation of noncollaborative working is to include information and explanation along with the invitation. This can give people a sense of control and choice, because they have enough information to make a decision about whether or not to take part. The dilemma may be about how much information is helpful in empowering people and how much may be constraining. Information that sets out goals and processes in definitive ways may create the impression that anyone who participates will have to think inside these constraints, so it needs to be made clear that the AI process will develop as it goes on and that new ideas will be encouraged and valued.

❖ AI PROCESSES OR CYCLES

The processes of AI have been envisaged as *cycles,* which have been developed in practice as practitioners have worked with different groups and organizations to develop directions for moving forward. The cyclical nature of the AI process points to the iterative nature of AI: It is not a linear process that starts and then stops when it is completed.

It is a process that never ends as the steps are repeated and organizations continue to learn and revisit phases in the process. Fitting in with the principles and assumptions of AI, the idea that questions change actions means that when the AI process is initiated, the changes can be integrated and sustained with the reflection that AI stimulates.

Cooperrider et al. (2003) cautioned, however, that AI should not be seen as just being made up of these cycles or processes—in other words, AI cannot be thought of as just a set of procedures. These cycles are an operationalization of AI thinking, but this stems from the AI way of thinking about change. One central idea is that of the "positive core," which has been described as "the greatest, yet least recognized, resource in the change management field" (Cooperrider et al., 2003, p. 30). This positive core is made up of the strengths, goals, and achievements of the organization—what gives it life—which may be expressed in many ways. This expression may be found in statements about the resources and practices of an organization, the stories that it tells about itself. Building on the positive core is the basis of AI—discovering and enhancing it—and is the way that AI can take an organization forward.

This discussion has emphasized the reflective nature of AI work; the processes of setting questions and approaches is a product of thoughtful responses to particular situations and contexts. At the same time, however, AI is not an anarchic process, in which all thinking is done as the work goes along and no boundaries are set. In the course of developing AI, some processes have been named that set out the stages or steps of AI, identifying markers for development that both facilitators and participants can use to assess progress. The two most common are the 4-D and the 4-I cycles, which are discussed below.

The *4-D cycle*, Coghlan et al. (2003) claimed, is the most often used AI framework, so it is presented first here. The other framework, the *4-I cycle*, is described next. The differences between the two are slight, so deciding which one to choose may be a matter of judgment, based on the particular context of the AI work and the preferences of the group and facilitator. Each one has the core concept of a circular or iterative process, and the differences lie in the way that the phases within are identified.

4-D Cycle

Discovery: Appreciating What Gives Life. In this phase, there is a quest to find out about the organization and what gives it its energy and nature.

This assumes that there is something that gives energy, but it may be that participants need time and encouragement to explore this fully—the negative often seems more vivid and important, while the positive can be neglected. Whitney (1998) described this phase as "a quest to fill the organization's conversations with talk of positive possibilities" (p. 317), and this quest can be difficult to embark on against a background of focusing on failure or deficit. This phase usually involves group members interviewing each other around the topic chosen (choosing the topic is described above and is sometimes described as integral to the discovery phase). This process of interviewing may involve participants working in pairs to interview each other, or it may involve other activities, such as group discussions or exercises, but the products of this phase will form the foundations for what follows.

Dreaming: Envisioning What Might Be. In this phase, participants work together to develop ideas of what the future might or could be. This means thinking creatively and thinking big, unrestricted by ideas about how the group has usually developed. This process builds on the outcomes of the Discovery phase, but it may require participants to drop the usual restrictions of resources and relationships, as thinking about future plans that won't cost much or will be welcomed immediately by everyone may put too many limits on ideas.

Designing: Determining What Will Be. In this phase, participants work together to craft plans for the future. In keeping with the challenging nature of AI, this process may involve producing *provocative propositions*, which are statements about what the organization wants to achieve. As Whitney (1998) described them, they are "intended to stretch the organization as it moves to realize them" (p. 317). Developing provocative propositions means thinking in a confident and assertive way. They may include phrases like "Everyone will . . ." or "There will always be . . ." These statements set out unequivocal ambitions, with no caveats or conditions.

Delivery: Planning What Will Be. Here, the energy moves toward action planning, working out what will need to happen to realize the provocative propositions. This means thinking about specific activities and actions and making commitments to tasks and processes. Again, this stage draws on previous stages, particularly the Discovery phase, in which possibilities are explored through the lens of past successes and achievements.

4-I Cycle

The 4-I cycle is very similar to the 4-D cycle, with the possible differences that there is more discussion of the preparation for AI work and the AI process is described in a way that suggests that it may be particularly useful when the facilitator feels that emphasis may need to be placed on getting the ideas across, rather than concentrating on action. Overall, however, the cyclical structure is very similar, with all phases building on each other and the entire process being seen as a continuous and ongoing one.

Initiate. In the first phase of the 4-I cycle, participants are introduced to the key ideas of AI and the process they will be part of. The basic structures for the project are decided or explored (for example, who will be in the core group and what their responsibilities and relationships will be) and also the resources needed and timeline are anticipated. The AI topic or focus is also determined.

Inquire. Here, initial interviews and discussions take place, and the AI interview agenda is developed around the chosen topic. This may take several stages of drafting and revising, perhaps with some piloting or testing, to make sure that the questions are asked in the right ways to get information that addresses the topic. The acceptability and intelligibility of the questions will also be explored. Time is spent interviewing the maximum number and range of people possible.

Imagine. Here, the data are brought together and collated, and themes are identified. This can involve as many participants as needed, in a process in which either a small group works on the data and consults the wider group or the wider group takes part in the entire process of collation. Provocative propositions are developed and validated with as many members of the team as possible.

Innovate. Here, the AI plans are developed with as many participants as possible. The plans are implemented and reviewed according to a preplanned schedule. This is not a mechanistic or finite process, in that it is carried out as an automatic step in the process, but it may be an ongoing process that undergoes further adaptation and debate, ultimately returning participants to the beginning of the cycle again.

The 4-D and the 4-I cycles may look like rigid, predetermined procedures, toolkits for change to be followed faithfully and without deviation. This is not the case, however, as both processes are more fluid and responsive than this, adapting to the situations that participants find themselves engaged in and to their preferences and priorities. This requires a level of expertise from the facilitator that allows him or her to make a judgment about the pace and content of activities, and this kind of expertise can be difficult to assess or demonstrate. As with many OD strategies, sometimes it is possible to see outcomes only after a period of time: If AI has had an impact, it might not be apparent for weeks, months, or years after the intervention. Moreover, if AI aims to create a <u>climate of appreciation</u>, this may be difficult to demonstrate; it is not always amenable to measurement or marking. This broad aim also gives rise to some of the criticisms of the AI processes: that it is ambitious to expect that such a focused intervention can make a wider difference to the way an organization works or that change can be sustained.

❖ AI QUESTIONS

These descriptions of AI processes in OD paint a picture of possible sequences of activity and give a feel for how the focus of the work might be chosen and potential participants selected for invitation. While this overview is important for understanding AI, it is also important that specific elements of the processes are explored, particularly the sorts of questions that get asked in AI. By looking at examples of specific questions, the ideas of principles, assumptions, and cycles are demonstrated and brought to life.

Cooperrider et al. (2003) gave some examples of possible AI questions that give the flavor of how AI work can proceed. They pointed to three types of questions: opening questions, questions centered around the topic, and concluding questions (p. 88). The following are some of their examples of opening questions or requests:

- Describe a "peak experience" or "high point."
- What are the things you value most about
  - Yourself?
  - The nature of your work?
  - Your organization? (Cooperrider et al., 2003, p. 88)

These opening questions are striking in the way that they establish the positive nature of the AI work and frame the conversation in a way that maintains this position. They may be difficult to answer, particularly if participants are more used to thinking about their problems or failings or have a reluctance to "boast" about what they do.

The topic questions continue along the same lines. Cooperrider et al. (2003) suggested that these should be questions "with lead-ins which assume the subject matter in the question already exists" (p. 90). The topic questions, therefore, should not ask people about possibilities, but about actualities, and Cooperrider et al. gave an example based on the topic of "positive change strategies," which starts as follows: "We have all been part of initiatives, large or small, where we have joined with others to create positive change, that is, change that brings ideas and dreams of better world into being" (p. 90). After this beginning, the questions can then go on to ask for accounts of experiences of positive change, having assumed that the participant has had them. This type of question does not ask for confirmation or speculation about whether the experience has happened, as conversations could end in the participant denying or decrying the experience, but goes straight on to exploring the details of the experience.

The concluding questions continue along the same lines, building on the positive stories that the participant has recounted and asking what the future might hold, given this experience. Cooperrider et al. (2003) suggested one question in particular that illustrates the way an AI question concludes by encouraging participants to move forward: "What three wishes do you have for changing the organization?" (p. 91). This question leaves people looking forward to the future by asking them to give a precise and well-thought-out response: The "three wishes" need to be defined and described in fairly detailed ways.

Cooperrider et al. (2003) gave general principles for crafting AI questions, which include thinking about questions as having two parts:

- Part A: The question must evoke a real personal experience and narrative story that help the participant to identify and draw on their best learning from the past.
- Part B: This part of the question allows the interviewer to go beyond the past to envision the best possibilities of the future.

By crafting questions in this way, the AI practitioner can root responses in actual experiences yet engage participants in new ways of thinking about these experiences and future possibilities.

❖ WAYS OF DOING OD: HOW AI FITS IN

The description of AI given above focuses on the ways in which it is different from other OD approaches, which start off with identifying problems in an organizational environment. As Johnson and Leavitt (2001) described, organizations have been bombarded with a huge range of different approaches to managing change and development, including total quality management (TQM), reengineering, and high-performance organization (HPO) philosophies (p. 129). Coghlan et al. (2003) mentioned a few more, including continuous quality improvement (CQI) and future search (FS) (p. 5). What these approaches have in common are ideas about processes of change that involve identifying problems, analyzing causes, and planning solutions. Many of these models have involved wide participation across organizational members, varying according to the strategy; this may involve distinct task groups or more general processes of involvement. Rather than the notion of a "line of command," in which managers tell people what to do and the effectiveness of the strategy rests on the salience and accuracy of the commands, there is a growing awareness that OD is shared: Everyone in the organization plays a part, not just the manager.

These ideas of cooperation have also been reflected in the way that ideas about leadership have changed, leadership being one way in which organizations can respond to challenges. While notions of autocratic leadership once predominated and prized qualities like decisiveness and charisma were powerful, these gave way to ideas about communicative skills and delegation ability (Horner, 1997). Instead of looking at the characteristics of leaders (one permutation of this is the "Leaders are born, not made" idea, in which leaders are viewed as having naturally occurring characteristics), attention turned to looking at what leaders did and how they did it. The next stage was to look at the contexts in which leaders act, and it became apparent that different contexts made actions more or less effective. This led to an increased interest in the interplay between leaders and contexts, both the internal contexts of organizational goals and systems and the external contexts of the world in which they operated. Taking this idea even further, McNamee and Gergen (1999) argued the case for moving away from notions of individual responsibility to ideas of "relational responsibility," which focus on relationship processes rather than the accountability and actions of isolated individuals (p. 6).

The trend in OD, therefore, has been to move away from what Hamel (2000) called "mechanistic" ideas about organizations, with associated ideas about rational planning based on adequate information about the world, to a much more organic idea of the complexity of organizations. Morgan (1997) also pointed to the prominence and power of the "machine" metaphor of organizations, describing the influence of "Taylorism," an early form of the mechanistic model of organizations that reduced work to a series of simplified steps (the idea of the "production line"), and an investigation of the "time and motion study"; both demonstrate a view of the world that denied and dismissed complexity (p. 25). Plsek and Wilson (2001) described this complexity using the example of health care organizations as they contrasted the management thinking that "assumes that a well-functioning organization is akin to a well-oiled machine" with the notion of an organization as "a complex adaptive system," within which the interactions are often more important than the discrete actions of the individual parts (p. 746). This shift in thinking has also prompted a reevaluation of ideas about change, as Nelson (2003) argued, moving from the notion of change as being "an aberration or departure from the more usual static position of organizations" to ideas about "dynamic models, reflecting the discontinuous nature of organizational change" (p. 18). Burnes (2004) argued that this represents a rereading of classic texts on change theory, notably the work of Kurt Lewin, who had been regarded as a theorist who portrayed change as a linear process with defined stages. Burnes suggested that the growing awareness of the complexity of change might make Lewin's theory outdated, but his reexamination of the work suggests that Lewin did address complexity and is as relevant as ever.

Overall, then, developments in thinking and theorizing about organizations and change fit with some of the basic concepts of AI. There is an emphasis on the importance of collaboration and participation across an organization in order to respond to drivers for change. This emphasis has also embraced external contexts, that is, the wider world in which an organization exists. The dynamic and continuous nature of change has also been recognized in OD thinking. All of these elements are reflected in AI, which emphasizes the following:

- Collaborative action: developing partnerships for change across and within groups
- Integrating whole systems of organizations and people: reaching consensus by inclusive and contextual working
- Future thinking and planning: embracing change

Where AI perhaps differs most vividly from other OD models is in its focus on strength-based approaches to change: It builds on "what works." While many other models focus explicitly or implicitly on problem identification and problem solving (see, for example, Knippen & Green, 1997), AI offers something different. In other approaches to OD, work begins with the idea of a deficit: The organization is failing or will fail to do something unless some OD work is done and a "fix" is found (Whitney, 1998). This is different from AI, in which the assumption is that organizations are achieving and this needs to be built on. The assumptions of AI, however, stretch beyond this starting position to ways in which AI processes can take place. Appreciating the abilities and strengths of colleagues and partners lays a foundation from which AI cycles and processes go ahead. Steps such as identifying peak experiences and thinking about dream futures become more possible if participants' capacities are recognized first. Furthermore, AI recognizes that it is an intervention that "causes ripples in the life of an institution" (Rogers & Fraser, 2003, p. 81). Doing AI not only facilitates development of plans for change but also alters the organization in which change takes place. The exercise of appreciating strengths has an impact beyond the exercise itself.

❖ CRITICISMS AND QUESTIONS FOR AI

A number of questions have, of course, been raised about AI, and not surprisingly, many of them concern its strengths-based orientation, the aspect that does seem to differ most from other approaches (Coghlan et al., 2003). AI has been accused of being naive and idealistic in the way that it concentrates on positive experiences, which some may feel paints an unduly sanitized picture of human life. Moreover, AI has been accused of focusing on positive aspects to the extent that it can ignore or suppress accounts of negative experiences.

There are a number of responses to these criticisms, ranging from the practical to the theoretical. McNamee (2003), for example, described how in using AI, she has found that "problems and weaknesses are often much easier to address when evaluation takes an appreciative stance" (p. 37). Difficulties can be discussed, and in an appreciative context, this can be facilitated when there is freedom from censure and blaming. The staff of Mountbatten Ward, Wright, and Baker (2005) found this particularly when using AI in the U.K. National Health Service (NHS). The organization, as the authors stated, was in a period of change in which there seemed to be "poor connection between NHS strategic and operational levels" and a focus on problem solving such that "the problem tends to be identified with individual(s) risking scapegoating" (p. 42). Using AI overcame this tension, and, as the authors described, led to high levels of participation. The positive approach of AI can be seen, therefore, as a factor that make discussions more open and possible.

Using AI in organizations in which stresses and pressures are high, like health services, does not mean that conversations avoid or ignore negative experiences. The experience of using AI in a number of studies suggests that interviews are negotiated, not imposed, and that if people want to talk about problems, they will. Sometimes this happens because the idea of AI is so new to people who have lived in a culture of faultfinding that it takes time for them to switch from a defensive way of responding to one that explores strengths. Images of research and researchers may be of punitive inquisitions, led by management, or experiences of previous OD initiatives may have been negative ones. In these contexts, conversations may need to address negative positions before they can move on to appreciating strengths.

These practical observations also point to some theoretical debates about AI, that is, the social constructionist framework that it draws upon. The social constructionist perspective will be discussed further in the next chapter, but here, it can be summarized as arguing that rather than focusing on trying to find the "truth" in the sense of objective fact, as in other ways of thinking about the world, looking at the ways in which people socially construct their world is a more useful way forward. This is because what would appear on first examination to be incontrovertible phenomena are subject to varying interpretations by the people who engage with them, and inquiring into the process of interpretation and construction goes to the heart of what is happening. For AI, then, the process of inquiry does not have to do with whether participants are factually accurate in their accounts, but rather with the idea that supporting them in exploring the positive can contribute to development in a different way.

Another criticism of AI is that it does not engage with issues of power, portraying the world as a benevolent place in which the possibilities for future action are unconstrained. This differs from many experiences of OD, in which issues of power and authority play a major part. The fact that an AI project is commissioned is an example of power in operation, as organizations find resources to engage in AI work. The power to facilitate can be withdrawn if the project does not go as the commissioners wish, and so participants may find or anticipate that the plans they make for the future will need to be approved, rather than automatically actioned. Similarly, power may influence the process of AI as participants interview each other and share ideas. Interviews between people wielding different forms of power may be shaped as much by this difference as by the aims of AI.

The debate about power illustrates a potential difficulty with the use of constructivist thought. If we take onboard the idea that the social world is constructed, this applies to power as well as other aspects of the social world, such as resources, roles, and responsibilities. While pointing to the element of construction in these areas might be a useful way of reexamining our thinking, we must also be careful not to deny the impact and effect on participants of these constructs.

This criticism perhaps points to a general consideration to be made when talking about any new approach, and that is, as Rogers and Fraser (2003) concluded, that we need to make sure that presentations of new approaches do not make "a straw man of other approaches or oversimplify the new approach" (p. 81). As Rogers and Fraser pointed out, there is a danger that arguments for AI rest on hostile evaluations of other approaches, or, as they stated,

> We suspect that Appreciative Inquiry could go dangerously wrong, leading to vacuous, self-congratulatory findings (by avoiding hard issues and uncomplimentary data): even worse, Appreciative Inquiry could provide a platform for airing vengeful and destructive sentiments by drawing implicit comparisons between ideal performance and performance of those present [other evaluators]. (pp. 80–81)

Bushe (2000) pointed to an additional question, that as AI becomes fashionable, what goes by that name may not even be faithful to the approach:

> Any inquiry that focuses on the positive in some way gets called Appreciative Inquiry. . . . The result will be that the unique power of this idea gets corrupted and lost and Appreciative Inquiry becomes just another discarded innovation on the junk heap of "failed" management effectiveness strategies. (p. 99)

This concern over authenticity is understandable, given (a) the popularity of AI and the many people who claim to use it and (b) Rogers and Fraser's (2003) point about the potential for justifying AI as being more effective than other OD approaches, which can be seen as concern about the way that AI itself develops, without rigor and transparency. Rogers and Fraser therefore concluded, "We do not need more narratives of the evaluator as hero" (p. 81). In other words, a critical understanding of AI needs to be developed, and this should go beyond anecdotes to a thorough exploration of the ways in which AI is practiced and the impact it has. For this book, there is another imperative: that we think through ways in which the principles of AI can be developed as an approach to research. As part of this thinking, the next chapter will explore ways in which AI links with other research methodology frameworks. This change of focus leads to debates about AI as a research methodology.

❖ IMPLICATIONS FOR RESEARCH

This summary of AI demonstrates some key features that can inform exploration so that it is reflective of this approach. Put simply, *AI focuses on supporting people getting together to tell stories of positive development in their work that they can build on.* This suggests a number of points to inform research:

> *Supporting people:* AI research needs to take an engaged stance rather than a disengaged one, as AI development is facilitated by the active input of those exploring change.

> *People getting together:* AI research is communal, in that it involves collective interaction to share and explore experiences.

> *Telling stories:* An interest in the "telling process," the language that people use to express ideas, is evoked in AI.

> *Positive development:* AI focuses on change and innovation and the generation of plans for the future. The process of development in AI starts with uncovering experiences of achievement in the past and present and involving people in planning for the future. This temporal dimension fits with notions of story and narrative.

> *Changes in the workplace:* AI emphasizes the importance of focusing on the workplace setting and understanding its context.

These points correspond to points made in AI discussions that seem to have clear implications for research, resonating with a range of different approaches and worldviews. While this link with research is made here in a particular way, it is not necessarily the only way that links can be made, and readers may well make different connections of their own to their experiences and understanding of research. Over the rest of the book, as research approaches and methods are explored in relation to AI, the possibilities of different connections should be borne in mind and arguments examined to determine whether they make sense: for example, where the gaps and emphases are and whether other viewpoints could have been taken. It was reported that Buddha, addressing an audience about his interpretation of the world, concluded by saying to them that they should not accept ideas because he had uttered them, but because, after careful reflection, the ideas made sense. This practice of *reflection* has resonance in this book: Please read it and come to your own decisions about what makes sense.

3

Research Frameworks

Where Does AI Connect With Research?

❖   ❖   ❖

This chapter builds on the last two chapters, which, first, described the initial encounters that I had with Appreciative Inquiry (AI) and, then, presented an overview of the development of AI, primarily as an organizational development (OD) strategy. As Bushe (1995) argued, "The technology of appreciative inquiry as a social research method and as an organization development (OD) intervention are evolving differently" (p. 14). From looking at these different evolutions, it seems that the OD technology has been developed much more—the volumes of books, papers, and presentations attest to this— while the evolution of AI as a research methodology seems to have progressed less in comparison.

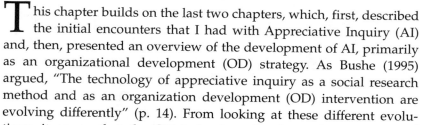 *OD has progressed more than AI research*

In this chapter and the next, the aim is to explore these ideas in more depth and to locate AI within the range of positions and ideas that research offers. This is not a simple process of slotting AI into a particular school of thought, as the fit is not as straightforward as that; rather, AI can be linked to a number of ideas and traditions across a range of methodologies, but it cannot be said to fit exclusively or exactly to any one school. In this way, AI could be said to show a "family resemblance" to different research models: It does not match any one exactly or exclusively, but shows different characteristics that can be related to a range of methodologies (Wittgenstein, 1967). This is not surprising, as AI is valued for its original and innovative approach to development, and it is this "newness" that makes AI a challenge to place in existing frameworks of research.

Mapping AI against these frameworks, however, is a process that offers a way of thinking through the implications of using it as a research approach, implications for organizing and carrying out AI studies. Looking at the key principles of these research models can offer a way of thinking about the ways in which AI research shares or differs from these principles and therefore what it is that AI research can offer in the development of knowledge and understanding. This is a challenging process, largely because the models in the world of OD and in the world of research differ in some ways, and so some issues may have to be described and explained differently in order to respect and respond to these different frameworks. Using AI as a tool for OD, for example, may require practitioners to think through issues around the *outcome* of what they do, that is, the effect on the organization and its practices. Using AI as a research method, however, may mean shifting the emphasis of thinking to the *processes* of inquiry, that is, the way in which information is gathered and interpreted. Whereas in OD, the main question may be "What effect did it have?" the question in AI research may be "How was it done?"

This is not to claim that research and OD are absolutely distinct and different ways of thinking. Research is simply one way, among many others, of trying to understand the world we live in. It is, however, a way that comes with a particular language, set of concerns, and areas of discussion that can seem unwelcoming. This chapter maps out some of these debates in a way that links with some of the debates in AI, in order to provide a context for discussion of AI as a research framework. The history of AI, as told in the previous chapter, includes research that shaped the ideas and practice of AI, but this was a research contribution primarily through the *findings* of research rather than the *methodology*. This chapter turns to the connections that can be made between research and AI through debates on methods (strategies for data collection) and methodology (principles of data collection). As Cooperrider and Whitney (1999) argued, AI has to do with asking questions, "the co-evolutionary search for the best in people, their organizations, and the relevant world around them" (p. 57).

It is useful here to revisit the points made at the end of the last chapter, in which the key features of AI were drawn out, as starting points for thinking about implications for research: *AI focuses on supporting people getting together to tell stories of positive development in their work that they can build on.* This gives a number of points to inform research:

Supporting people: AI research needs to take an engaged stance rather than a disengaged one, as AI development is facilitated by the active input of those exploring change.

People getting together: AI research is communal, in that it involves collective interaction to share and explore experiences.

Telling stories: An interest in the "telling process," the language that people use to express ideas, is evoked in AI.

Positive development: AI focuses on change and innovation and the generation of plans for the future. The process of development in AI starts with uncovering experiences of achievement in the past and present and involving people in planning for the future. This temporal dimension fits with notions of story and narrative.

Changes in the workplace: AI emphasizes the importance of focusing on the workplace setting and understanding its context.

This summary has some clear messages for research development if this is to grow from and reflect the use of AI as a tool for OD, and the following pages outline some research approaches that can reflect and enhance the use of AI in research. If AI is to be developed as a research tool, it is useful to know and understand the historical and philosophical contexts of different research approaches, so that this development can be thoughtful and considered. This leads back to the elements of AI outlined above, which have been drawn from the debates about AI in OD. In the context of research traditions, this raises many issues, both in terms of the best way to do this (i.e., issues of method) and how this connects to debates about validity (i.e., issues of methodology). In other words, there are not only technical issues concerning how to explore ideas and information but also theoretical issues concerning what this information is about. This chapter will set out these debates in order to place AI in the context of research development, not trying to "fit" AI into research methodologies or, indeed, fit research methodologies into AI, but to point to the connections that can be made between the two and how they can inform each other.

A central argument of this book is that AI is not only an OD approach, useful for taking organizations forward, but that it also has the potential to contribute to research-derived knowledge, in ways that stem from the observation that its methodology can serve to place other research findings and methodological debates in sharper focus. In this way, AI can contribute toward knowledge both in the way that it asks and explores different sorts of questions about the world and in the way it can challenge ideas about methodology. This is not a one-way process, however, because many of the discussions in research can enhance clarity and transparency in some of the debates in OD. These debates, both in research and in OD, are about what we mean when we say that we "know" something, either as we respond to it to develop a plan for an organization or when we present our research contributions to theoretical knowledge and understanding. An exploration of this "knowing" starts with an overview of the historical and philosophical contributions to the debate.

❖ NOTIONS OF "SCIENCE," "TRUTH," AND "FACT"

A key theme running through discussions of research methodologies is the debate about ideas and definitions of *truth* and, following from these definitions, how it can be established. In the final chapter of this book, definitions of truth will be revisited in the context of debates about theoretical development, but here, the idea of "truth" is discussed as the driver for ideas about research methods. One very powerful model of truth is that it is about "facts," or objectively observed phenomena, and that science is the only way to find them—everything else is speculation, opinion, or feeling. Thus, the processes and methods of "science" are defined in precise terms and carried out in a publicly authorized and validated way. The images from history of the discovery of phenomena are mainly stories about methods and results, how experiments or surveys were carried out and produced findings that led to new knowledge and understanding as they contributed to theoretical frameworks. The notion of *scientific truth* here is a collaborative one; it is based on the work of a community of scientists who can pool their work, because it follows the same rules of process and presentation.

This model of science, fact, and truth is a very narrow and somewhat sanitized one—it draws tight boundaries between what is and is not science and what the proper goals and results of science should be (Midgley, 1989, 1992). As Kuhn (1970) argued, this is a characteristic of science: It has shared rules about how to go on. Moreover, he goes on to state,

Effective research scarcely begins before a scientific community thinks it has acquired firm answers to questions like the following: What are the fundamental entities of which the universe is composed? How do they interact with each other and the senses? What questions might legitimately be asked about such entities and what techniques employed in seeking solutions? . . . Answers to questions like these are firmly embedded. (Kuhn, 1970, p. 4)

In other words, these questions can be taken to characterize a body of science and its accompanying assumptions about legitimate goals and procedures: its paradigm. Kuhn's notion of "paradigm shift" holds that the internal consistency of a paradigm comes under pressure as contradictory arguments challenge it, and then there is an abrupt and extreme move to another paradigm, with new assumptions.

Kuhn: paradigm shift

Kuhn's analysis can, and has, been challenged as proposing a linear model of development, with new paradigms replacing old ones, one challenge being that this does not necessarily reflect the way in which some paradigms overlap or coexist (happily or not) within the broad enterprise of inquiry. Nonetheless, it is sometimes useful to think about research traditions as being paradigms, with consistency across the goals and methods that each paradigm values, as long as we don't get too rigid in our thinking and assume that boundaries around paradigms are impermeable and inflexible. The world of scientific debate is looser than this.

research traditions as paradigms

It is possible, however, to identify two basic sets of ideas of what research is about, using the concept of paradigms. As Holliday (2002) commented, this is a common way to begin discussions of research, although it is an "unadventurous way to begin, but necessary, because when asked, 'What is research' most people refer to the more familiar, traditional quantitative research" (p. 1). For the sake of simplicity, here, I will follow Holliday's terminology and call them the *quantitative* and the *qualitative research paradigms*, although a huge range of different terms have been and are being used. Both have been called various names at various times—names that in themselves reflect particular debates and traditions, and these include positivism and deductive theory development, on one hand, and interpretive and inductive theory development, on the other.

This interest in what could be known has also been connected with a concern with what could be known *with certainty*, that is, what could remain unchanged. This came out of early recorded Greek philosophy, particularly that of Plato, in which views of truth were founded on its supposed unchanging nature: If something were transient, then it could not be true, as it was changeable and varied over time, whereas truth had to have an eternal nature, according to Plato. This search for certainty excluded practical knowledge; as something that responded to circumstances and contexts, practical knowledge could not be certain and therefore based on truth. Descartes (1641/1960) similarly identified the inaccessibility of the world through the senses and concluded that the only thing he could be certain of was that he was thinking. Everything else could be a delusion or an error, a position that accorded more certainty to the intellectual world than the physical.

More recently, however, philosophical discussions about truth have been shaped by *pragmatist philosophy*, sometimes summed up in the statement that "truth is what works," an approach that does include practical knowledge. While this summary may seem a little too sweeping to be rigorous, the drivers for pragmatism came from a disenchantment with abstract philosophical debates that treated ideas of truth as being disconnected from everyday experiences. Pragmatism, therefore, proposed that these abstract definitions of truth should be discarded in favor of a focus on what knowledge made possible. An example would be the knowledge of how to ride a horse, which would make travel possible. Critics, however, would challenge this measure of knowledge, particularly on the grounds that much about reality is not known or is not immediately evident but this does not mean that it is not true. An example would be the curvature of the Earth's surface, which is not evident through direct observation, but makes a difference to the way travel is undertaken—not least because horses and riders would fall off the edge of a flat earth. Pragmatists, however, would contend that this was a measure of the value of the knowledge, in that the more that was known, the more able people were to direct their activities. While pragmatism was and is not a unanimous school of thought, more recent developments can be usefully summarized by reference to the work of Rorty (1999):

> We cannot regard truth as a goal of inquiry. The purpose of inquiry is to achieve agreement among human beings about what to do, to bring consensus on the end to be achieved and the means to be used to achieve those ends. Inquiry that does not achieve co-ordination of behaviour is not inquiry but simply word play. (p. xxv)

Here, we can see the pragmatist skepticism about abstract notions of truth and a concern with knowledge that guides action. As Reason (2003) argued, this makes a link between pragmatism and action research. By extending this idea to other forms of research that have change as a goal, the links to AI are also evident.

In the discussions that follow, of quantitative and qualitative research paradigms, these ideas about knowledge should be borne in mind as a context for the models of what can be known and how it can be discovered.

❖ QUANTITATIVE RESEARCH

Investigations into the world of nature grew rapidly, as scientists explored physical phenomena such as the solar system, animal and plant life, and the processes of motion. This science involved the careful observation and quantitative measurement of phenomena in the natural world, from the movements of the planets to the reproduction of animals and plants. While much of this effort faced hostility from those who saw scientific investigations as disrespectful to established ways of thinking, nonetheless knowledge grew, and the ways of investigation *Enlightenment* grew too, with tools and methods becoming more precise and reliable. This included not only developing ways of observing and recording phenomena but also ways of organizing research, so that ideas could be developed. In this way, theoretical propositions or hypotheses would be formulated in a way that made them testable, and interventions and observations would be sequenced in ways that allowed the data to be analyzed in order to support or disconfirm the hypothesis.

Similarly, attention gathered on the social world and the possibility of its exploration using the methods of the natural sciences. These methods offered some advantages in the pursuit of knowledge, and, importantly, they came from a scientific tradition with well-established rules and procedures. In this way, research debates about, for example, the reliability of measures, generalization to wider populations, and sampling strategies were shaped by debates in the physical sciences and, in turn, shaped the social sciences. One central tenet of the physical sciences, for example, was proposed by Popper (1963), who argued that scientific knowledge proceeded through the process of falsification; that is, scientific theories were formulated in testable terms, and efforts were made to falsify them. If this effort succeeded, the theory was rejected, and if it failed, efforts could continue using different approaches. A theory could never be fully verified, as the next study could overturn it. What the Popperian model said was that theories could, therefore, only be *provisionally* accepted. This idea reflected and strengthened the way that physical research was formulated, as a series of testable hypotheses, and these conventions were also sometimes applied to social research as criteria it should aspire to meet.

This movement, whereby the principles of the physical sciences were applied to the investigation of the social world and its structures, has been given many names, depending on the stories told about origins and histories (Silverman, 1985). As indicated above, I will call it *quantitative research* here, as an accessible term, although appreciating that it does not do justice to the complexities of this paradigm. As has been pointed out, a number of questions were raised about its validity. Was the social world such a matter of interpretation and perspective that quantitative approaches would fail to capture, and indeed ignore, the ambiguities that were of most interest?

❖ QUALITATIVE RESEARCH

From this concern, a range of other approaches developed, which I will call *qualitative research.* These include approaches that concentrated on processes of discovery and description in ways that did not look at the quantity of phenomena (e.g., number and extent of occurrences), but at the quality of the experience (e.g., thoughts and feelings about it). Hence, a range of approaches developed, from the very broad, such as *ethnography* (the describing of the cultures of the people being studied in a range of different dimensions), to the specific, such as *life history methodology* (in which people are invited to present the stories of their lives and their ideas of chronology and causality). Holliday (2002) offered a more detailed discussion of the qualitative paradigm and its central interests.

Stimulated in part by concerns about quantitative approaches, qualitative approaches offered a different way of exploring the social world. Early work from the "Chicago school" of research, for example, explored naturally occurring behaviors and events. This work was carried out without recourse to some of the central tenets of quantitative research. It did not try to control events (as in experimental design or controlled sampling processes), and it used responsive and unstructured methods (such as living alongside people and recording what was seen and discussed). As Bobasi, Jackson, and Wilkes (2005) argued, however, early qualitative work still maintained a distant "scientific" stance, following orthodox research traditions (de Laine, 2001), and "because of its 'objectivity,' the resulting ethnographic account was deemed a 'true' reflection of the reality or way of life of those under observation" (Bobasi et al. 2005, p. 494). As Bobasi et al. (2005) went on to describe, however, examination of these assumptions has resulted in more engaged and personal approaches to fieldwork.

This work moved away from the sort of questions asked in quantitative research, such as "How much?" and "How often?" and began to ask questions about the quality of experiences, or what people thought and felt. This approach also moved away from exploring theories through hypothesis testing to inductive theory development, in which, from unstructured data collection, ideas and concepts emerge. The idea of inductive theory development was tellingly articulated by Glaser and Strauss (1967), in the book in which they discussed the process of developing theory that was "grounded" in empirical data rather than abstract ideas.

❖ WHERE DOES AI FIT?

The discussion above gives an overview of paradigms in research, that is, the positions of quantitative and qualitative research. It sets up a dichotomy that may not always be very helpful: It suggests clear *False* differences between the positions, whereas in practice, the boundaries *Dichotomy* are not always so sharply defined. Furthermore, it would not necessarily be useful if they were sharply defined—we would be tempted to put research approaches in boxes and close the lid on them. We may feel, after looking at the ambiguities and overlaps between the models, that we can see a set of "family relationships," to return to Wittgenstein's ideas, first mentioned in the introduction to this chapter. There are resemblances and differences between the models that do not constitute a set of defining and distinguishing characteristics, but which nonetheless enable us to identify important features and the extent to which they are displayed in each model (Wittgenstein, 1967).

From this, AI can be placed across the range of quantitative and qualitative approaches. There is an interest in AI in how people feel and think about what they do and also the possibility that change might be evaluated by using quantitative measures. One example is provided by the study by the Staff of Mountbatten Ward, Wright, and Baker (2005). In this project, AI was used as a tool for staff development in a situation where low morale had been first identified alongside a high sickness level. The description of the project uses qualitative accounts to describe the processes that the staff engaged in and their responses to them—qualitative data. In addition, however, the project took into account levels of sickness as demonstrated by the counts of days absent from work—a quantitative measure. Another example is offered by Stevenson (1995), who used single-case design to evaluate family therapy with one family. Quantitative data were analyzed here,

though the study was not interested in generalizing to a larger population, but in examining the specific circumstances of one case.

Similarly, the design of AI projects can demonstrate resonance with
quantitative and qualitative processes. In many AI projects, things are
"tried out" and the consequences examined, which comes somewhere
near to the idea of formal experimentation from quantitative research.
Where AI would differ, however, would be that the experimentation
would be led by participants rather than the researcher, who, in orthodox experimental designs would, for example, randomly allocate
participants to different intervention groups and tightly control their
activities. The AI design would be unlikely to involve this level of control, and interventions would be consensual rather than imposed, but
it might still involve planned changes, the main difference being that
these would not be determined before the project began (as in an experiment), but would be formulated and planned as the project developed.
The project would include experimental elements, in the sense that
approaches would be tried and evaluated, but the emphasis would
be on evolving and shared design rather than predetermined testing.
While AI might involve some numerical or quantitative data, then, it
would not involve the control of events and environments needed
to carry out experimentation. It would be focused around a particular
naturally occurring group or context rather than aim to make general-
izations about wider populations.

In these ways, AI can be viewed as not belonging exclusively
to the quantitative or qualitative camp: available data can be collected
through AI activity. For this book, however, making links with research
methodologies is a useful way forward in the way that it can help us to
explore debates about AI as a research methodology, and so some connections have been made and will be discussed in the following pages.
Reviewing AI literature suggests that the research frameworks that
most closely reflect the central interests of AI are qualitative, in the
sense that they deal with "naturally occurring" phenomena rather than
controlled experimentation, and they are more open-ended, rather
than structured, in the data they collect. This is not to say that AI
research vehemently rejects quantitative research, but that some of the
central tenets of this, such as researcher-determined design, do not fit
comfortably with AI, which has developed in a way more responsive
to and directed by the ideas of participants. The following summary of
research models, therefore, covers social constructionist research and
critical theory as fundamental worldviews with significance for AI
research, and then it goes on to discuss the specific methodologies

of ethnography and case studies, narrative methodology, and action research.

❖ WORLDVIEWS

Some research worldviews display fundamental ideas about the way life goes on and what things are important to explore. The two indicated here are *social constructionist theory* and *critical theory*, which reflect central ideas in AI as they were presented at the end of the last chapter and the beginning of this one: the interest in how people can get together to story their world, to construct their thinking about it.

Social Constructionist Research

Central links can be made between AI and social constructionist research in the way that they share some concepts, namely, the notions of worlds as negotiated and co-constructed. This has been expressed in AI as the principle of *constructivism*, discussed in the previous chapter, and has been reiterated by Cooperrider and Whitney (1999). Gergen (1999) was one of the first writers to describe this approach and the ways in which it contrasted with established models of discovery and explanation. His work reflected some of the debates that this chapter began with, about the nature of truth. Gergen pointed to the challenges that had been made to the idea that the truth is arrived at by a rational and value-free process of discovery, challenges that stretched back to the work of Mannheim in the 1930s, when ideas about subjective experiences of the social world began to be detailed. The importance of these kinds of experiences was more than just an interesting facet of human life, as they suggested ideas about how these feelings and ideas could be developed to form constructions of the social world that could have a key role in shaping activity and understanding.

Burr (1995, pp. 3–5) listed some of the key principles of social constructionism:

• "A critical stance toward taken-for-granted knowledge" includes the idea that when we observe the world, our observations give us a straightforward and unproblematic understanding of the world. Social constructionism argues that much of the understanding we have of the world is a reflection of our perceptions of it. For example, when we feel that we know the difference between a civilized and a primitive society, what we are reflecting is a set of socially constructed assumptions about what these terms signify, rather than anything in the nature of different societies. In AI, this critical stance is demonstrated by the way AI encourages us to ask questions that challenge assumptions about the way things happen.

- "Historical and cultural specificity" suggests that the way we understand the world is not universal, but arises from the society in which we live and the cultural experiences we have shared. In AI work, then, the ideas that participants have about their world are acknowledged to be specific to the history and culture that we are part of or aware of, and so each project will be shaped by the cultural context in which it is situated.

- "Knowledge is sustained by social processes" emphasizes the importance of social processes in the construction of knowledge by people together, through their interactions and communications. This emphasis on the collective nature of knowledge is echoed in many AI processes in which groups get together to explore their understandings, for example, in paired interviews or group discussions. The processes of describing what has worked to each other and then going on to develop plans for the future together reflects the understanding not only that knowledge is developed through social interaction but also that knowledge developed in this way can shape social interaction. In other words, we come to an understanding of the world through our interactions with each other, such as when we produce descriptions of successful activity in AI, and these understandings support the action we take—the strategies we develop for the future.

- "Knowledge and social action go together" points to the way in which developing an understanding of the world changes not only the way we think and feel but also the way we act and behave. Once we know the world in a certain way, we act accordingly in ways that reflect and fit in with this knowledge. In AI work, the cycles of reflection and activity go together: If we start to appreciate our strengths, this will affect the way we move forward.

Many of these points about constructionist thought relate very closely to the principles of AI, particularly the emphasis on the way that people can shape their world through the way they talk and think about it. This is not to say that the world is just something we thought up, with no other dimensions, but it does point to the possibilities for change.

Critical Theory

Critical theory is a somewhat loose term and, as Fontana (2004) pointed out, draws on the work of a diverse group of thinkers whose commonality lies in the way they have challenged the established social order. This can and has involved taking the position of those whom the established way of thinking has excluded or oppressed. The links to AI lie in the way this challenges assumptions of inadequacy, by focusing on the positive achievements of people who can be regarded as powerless: the people who carry out the work of an organization.

Critical theory, then, focuses on reexamining established ideas in a way that is independent of the power structures that perpetuate them. An example would be a structure in which racial differences are used to support and are supported by differences in economic and social power. The example of Marxist inquiry has been given earlier in this chapter, and others associated with this critical stance are Habermas, a German philosopher, and Paulo Freire, a Brazilian writer.

Many other associations can be seen with some of the approaches outlined above, particularly social constructionism, which similarly questions the idea that knowledge can be a self-evident product of rational processes, and hermeneutics, which explores the processes of interpretation of accounts and expressed thoughts. What critical theory argues more strongly than these approaches, however, is that the role of inquiry is to challenge and critically evaluate these processes in a way that can emancipate participants from the restrictions that these ideas can entail.

For AI, then, critical theory can provide a useful addition to the practices of AI in the way that it can stimulate reflection. This can happen in the following ways:

- Critical theory can prompt AI projects to reflect on the taken-for-granted images of organizations and activities that participants may have. This can be in the way that questions are formulated or data interpreted.

- Critical theory can sensitize people doing AI to issues of power. While other models may suggest that power is an artifact of interpretation and can be countered by paying attention to different ways of thinking about the world, critical theory prompts taking issues of power as being strong shapers and drivers of the social world. In AI consultation, issues of the commissioning process, such as who decided and funded the AI work and power differences within the group activity, need to be taken into consideration in the way that activities are planned, carried out, and reported on.

❖ SPECIFIC METHODOLOGIES:
    EXPLORING CONTEXT AND DEVELOPMENT

The frameworks identified above point to the way in which AI research can draw from social constructionism and critical theory to explore and shape the ways the world can be explored. In addition to these world-views, however, more specific methodologies can also contribute to this understanding through paying attention to the context in which actions take place and the way in which change can happen, features that were identified at the beginning of this chapter as being key points for methodology to address.

Context and Place

The points presented at the beginning of this chapter summarized the central features of AI work and how this could inform practice. This included the features of the context of development, that is, the features of the environment and of the people who shaped activity. While there are a number of ways of exploring this context, two particular methodologies seem particularly appropriate in the way that they can inform research.

Ethnography

The term *ethnography* covers a range or a family of approaches that take their emphases from the concept of *ethno,* or "people." In short, these approaches seek to explore the salience of culture and society in the lives of the people studied. There are a number of related models, such as ethnomethodology and anthropology, each with different foci and methodological concerns. Atkinson, Coffey, Delamont, Lofland, and Lofland (2001) described contemporary ethnography as being notable for "fragmentation and diversity" (pp. 2–3). Not comfortable with this position, however, Gubrium and Holstein (1999) suggested that researchers "embrace confusion and experiment with an intermix-ing of voice, social conditions and authorial aspirations" (p. 571).

Silverman (1985) described the general concerns of ethnography as "the everyday practices through which (societal) 'members' make vis-ible ('observable-reportable') the orderly character of social relations"

(p. 95). The everyday practices may be concerned with language or behavior, but we can see parallels with AI that are concerned with making social relations visible in a particular way, by articulating what is seen as the best, or most successful, in what people do. While ethnography may not have the same focus on the best that AI has, it does have the focus on firsthand contact to explore cultures and ideas (Gubrium & Holstein, 1999) and a concern with research to "uncover, make accessible, and reveal the meanings (realities) people use to make sense out of their daily lives" (Jorgensen, 1989, p. 15).

Discussions in the field of ethnography sensitize us to many issues in the use of AI as a research methodology. These can be summarized as follows:

- *A focus on sense making and the nature of accounts.* What AI does is ask people to make sense of their world in a way that might be very different from the way that they have done in other contexts, a process that is important in ethnography. This may mean that participants move away from concentrating on identifying and examining problems to exploring achievements. This is not simply information about a different topic, but is information arrived at through a different process of thinking. This form of sense making can impact lives away from the AI study, in that it can shape sense making in everyday activities and has the potential to change activity across the research setting. In this way, AI faces two challenges: to support people in making sense of their world in what might be very different ways and to be alert to ways in which these different ways of thinking may affect other facets of life.

- *Ways to access accounts.* As mentioned above, eliciting AI accounts may involve a very different way of thinking. This can present issues similar to those encountered in ethnographic studies. Here, the goal is to make what are unrecognized processes of sense making more visible, to the degree that they can be recognized and presented. The processes of sense making may have become so habitual and familiar that the ethnographer has to be very supportive and encouraging to participants through the process of surfacing the "taken for granted." Similarly, the process of AI can involve challenging and examining habitual ways of focusing on problems and failures and shift attention to taken-for-granted achievements and positive aspects of activity.

- *Interest in the diversity and complexity of the social world.* In ethnography, there is a concern with mapping out the complexity of the social world, evident in anthropological field work. This would mean that the ethnographic researcher would be ready to explore aspects of the social world as and when their salience became apparent through interactions with research participants. In a similar way, the AI researcher may start with an area of interest but needs to flexibly follow the directions shown by participants as they talk about their activities, relationships, ideas, and feelings. An AI study can begin with a broad focus, but as more data are collected and more is discovered, other areas of investigation and sources of information can develop as the complexity of the social world becomes apparent in a way that it could not at the beginning of the study.

Case Study Methodology

Another research model that has links to AI and the exploration of context is *case study methodology*, in which discrete settings and groups are treated as being usefully defined and studied as whole entities. Yin (1984), a key writer on case study work, described the case study as being an approach to empirical enquiry that "investigates a contemporary phenomenon within its real-life context, when the boundaries between phenomenon and context are not clearly evident" (p. 13).

This definition points to some of the features of case study methodology. First, there is the emphasis on the contemporary nature of the phenomenon; second, there is the importance placed on its "real-life" nature; and, finally, and most important, there is the idea that a division between the setting and the phenomenon is difficult to draw—the phenomenon is intimately connected to the context and to research. One without the other would produce only a partial account of what is happening.

Case study research, then, is about treating the phenomena being researched as a distinct entity or case and exploring it in the context in which it occurs. This, however, does not tell us what a case is or how this can be demarcated, so a further definition is needed in order to concentrate inquiry on the questions being asked. This is quite a difficult move to make, paradoxically, because the links between phenomena and context that are so integral to the justification of using a case study approach also make it difficult to put boundaries around a case for the purposes of definition. Yin (1984) suggested that a case can be defined at a number of levels, ranging from an individual to an organization or sector, depending on the question being asked. Similarities with AI work are clear: Any efforts to explore, build on, or develop organizational practice will need to take into account the bounded nature of this practice, the context, and the characteristics of the organization. Specifically,

- The process of defining the case in AI is one that each researcher needs to engage with; in other words, the definition of a case needs to be thought through carefully in light of the research goals of the study. This may mean that a case is defined as an organization, a network, a practice, or an individual, to mention but a few of the possible definitional dimensions. The important part of the definition is its utility, which serves to direct data collection and analysis so that boundaries and parameters are clear. Defining the case, then, can be seen as a process not reliant on universal rules and procedures, but on the specific aims and focus of the research.

[handwritten margin notes: How to define the case / definition is built on utility]

- Case study definitions can be determined before work starts or as an organic development as work progresses. The process of definition, therefore, is part of the process of understanding the world in which the case exists. This is a process of thinking through in which, for the purpose of the study, the parameters of a case may be set. This may start as a fairly circumspect focus, stimulated by the debates around the beginning of involvement, as interests are developed and invitations issued, but it may change as more is known of the dynamics and dimensions of activity. A department within an organization may initially be defined as the case, but as more becomes known about it, this may change. The salience of other departments or other organizations may become evident, or what was first seen as a homogenous department may need to be diverse and usefully divided into constituent parts.

The purpose of the process of demarcation is to allow identification of the entirety of data collection and analysis in light of the research questions. Data will be collected across the entirety of the case in all its dimensions and will be analyzed in order to identify themes across these dimensions.

Development and Time/Change

In addition to the salience of context, the points presented at the beginning of this chapter included an appreciation of the temporal processes of change and development. Two methodologies have clear relevance to this issue. The first, narrative methodology, relates to the idea of storying experiences and ideas, while the second, action research, addresses points about the processes of development in work places.

Narrative Methodology

A form of research that resonates with AI methodology and the exploration of how change can happen is *narrative methodology,* which is research that elicits stories and accounts from participants. Narrative methodology, as in ethnography, is a way of exploring the world as the research participant explains it, but in narrative methodology, the way of understanding this is by involving the participant in the construction of a story, a telling of a pattern or series of events with elements of sequence and causality explored in the telling. This "storying" displays the connections being made between phenomena, and these stories are an element of AI inquiry, which asks not just about what is being appreciated but also about what helped it to happen and possibilities for the future. This is reflected in the discussion of the *poetic principle* of AI in the last chapter, the way people author their stories, reflecting their interests and goals. There are also features shared with the *anticipatory principle,* the way that the stories people author open the way to future actions.

Narrative methodology is one term that denotes methodology based on chronological accounts of events but in itself is not a term that evokes the personalized, individual nature of these accounts. This is perhaps more clearly evoked by the terms *biographical methods* and *life history methodology,* in which the interest is in eliciting accounts of participants' personal experiences over time. When looking at a person's experiences working for an organization, for example, the interest would not be on levels of qualification at entry, salary scale, or years of service, as it might be in a quantitative study, but the person's account of coming to work there and his or her experiences over time. Similarly, when looking at experiences in AI methodology, there is an interest in personal accounts. The links between AI and narrative approaches can be summarized as follows:

- Both AI and narrative methodology have an interest in *perceived chronology* or sequence of events, the way that participants report on the order in which events have happened. While this is not scrutinized to establish accuracy, it paints a picture of the way that participants view the central "plot" of an activity, for example, as a triumph over adversity or as a defeat by hostile forces. These plots can shape the ways participants see the future as well as the past.

- Linked to the notion of chronology is the idea of *causality*, what participants feel has driven the plot. These may be internal or external dynamics (the relationships with other people and organizations), and they may be deliberate or accidental. Again in AI, these ideas of causality are not examined or tested for factual accuracy, but for they way they can be evoked to develop ideas and explanations for the way things are and the way they might be.

Action Research

Perhaps the most obvious link between AI, research, and change is the connection with *action research*, a long-established form of inquiry that rejected some traditions of research, namely, the disengagement of the researcher from the world being researched. As Reason (1994) described, the idea that research should entail researchers standing back from the research setting, once viewed as a hallmark of the research effort, began to give way to a more involved stance. What became known as the *Hawthorne experiments* of the 1920s and 1930s showed that this was an impossible position to take; researchers would have an effect on the environment even when they made efforts to remain detached (Mayo, 1933). In the Hawthorne studies, researchers found that merely their presence in the workplace changed levels of production. Given that this effect would occur in any case, some researchers made the decision to make use of it and to engage explicitly with change, the process that became known as action research, particularly as it was explored by Kurt Lewin in the 1940s (Lewin, 1948). Even earlier than this, research had been used as a means of changing thinking, for example, in the work of Marx (1858/1973), who asked workers about their wages and the price of the products they manufactured in factories, to stimulate awareness of anomalies between price rises and wage reductions. The idea of research as having an impact on action, of being an intervention in itself, is also reflected in the AI principle of *simultaneity*, discussed in the last chapter.

Action research has been explored and developed as a way of building on the potential synthesis of research and change. It was defined by Kemmis and McTaggart (1998) as follows:

A form of collective enquiry undertaken by participants in social situations in order to improve the rationality and justice of their own social or educational practice, as well as their understanding of these practices and the situations in which these practices are carried out. (p. 5)

This definition emphasizes the collective and participatory nature of action research and also its key aims: to inform and change practice and develop understanding of the particular context in which it takes place. This involves a number of research processes, namely, the development of the research questions and design in a collaborative way across the research setting, iterative processes of data collection and analysis, and the feeding back of the results of the analysis into the setting to stimulate change. This cycle of data collection, analysis, feedback, and change may be carried out several times and, indeed, may become an integral part of the practice environment. Connections between action research and AI can be seen in the interest in observing and promoting change. The main difference is that while AI begins by finding out about the achievements of an organization, action research typically has a problem-solving focus. It begins by identifying a problem and then works out solutions to it. From this, the cycle of planning change, implementing strategies, and evaluating the effects bears a strong resemblance to the AI cycle of "Dreaming, Designing, and Delivering."

Action research also links with AI in its concern with organizational dynamics and power. Organizational dynamics can shape the course of an action research project as much as in AI work: Both have to develop a supportive and open relationship between the researcher and participants. This enables participants to feel safe in talking about their work and developing strategies for taking it forward. Both types of research also need to pay attention to dynamics outside the immediate group, so that the work will be supported and not sabotaged by others. This involves an understanding of issues such as power, responsibility, and communication, in that if these are not negotiated, projects can find themselves blocked or promoted in ways that are not helpful.

A model of change that is cyclical rather than linear is evident in action research and AI. Rather than the process of development going from investigation to implementation to evaluation and then finishing, the impact of the exploration is anticipated to continue for some time, as the participants become aware of the potential impact of thinking and acting differently. Similarly. In AI, the 4-D and 4-I cycles can continue past any specific intervention to become part of people's lives.

Engagement between researcher and participant is seen as a fundamental part of action research. The idea of *engagement,* that the act of carrying out research has an intended and acknowledged effect on the world being researched, contrasts with other models of research that would see this as "contamination," to be avoided or minimized. In AI, engagement is also acknowledged: in OD work as a fundamental basis of working for change and in research as a foundation for exploration and understanding. This moves research away from being simply an exercise in observing events to what Reason and Torbert (2001) called "transformational social science," in which the role of research is also to facilitate change.

❖ CONCLUSION

The connections between the different research models can be usefully summarized as in Table 3.1. This summary does, of course, simplify

Table 3.1   Connections Between Models of Research and AI

Model	Links to AI	Concerns
Worldview		
Social constructionism	Concern with meaning and interpretation rather than measurable facts	Ensuring that the meanings the world has for participants are understood
Critical theory	Interest in developing challenges to ways of thinking	Searching for data that question assumptions
Context		
Ethnography	Interest in complexity of the social world and understanding it in its entirety	Collecting diverse forms of naturally occurring data that encompass the social world
Case studies	Focus on specific settings or situations	Determining the boundary of the case
Change		
Narrative methodology	Interest in hearing stories of events and processes	Ensuring that stories are told and heard and that ideas of chronology are explored
Action research	Interest in facilitating change	Following the processes of change

these models, bypassing the subtlety and complexity of much of the discussion and thinking behind them. Nonetheless, this simplification does allow some of the central features of each model to be identified and linked to AI.

Table 3.1 points to some of the links that can be made between research approaches and AI methodology, and it indicates the chief concerns of these research models. This gives an overview of potential connections, and readers may well make links of their own, but the left-hand column is of most interest here: The chief methodological concerns of each model are outlined, in other words, what people using this approach are concerned about addressing. Each model has a long and sometimes complex history, and so the discussion has been necessarily short, concentrating on what the models may offer the development of AI as a research framework. Connections can be seen, however, with AI research, and this points to bodies of discussion and writing that can be explored further to follow up particular methodological issues.

This short tour of theoretical and methodological positions and their potential links to AI work has been necessarily brief and has run the risk of oversimplifying positions (all of which have extensive literature and texts) or of missing some altogether. Bearing these limitations in mind, this chapter has sought to give a flavor of these ways of thinking and to draw out links with AI. In the AI literature available, these links between theory and practice have been made mostly with the practice of AI as an OD strategy rather than as a research methodology. This, then, is the task for this book: to explore ways in which the theoretical frameworks that have given impetus and life to AI as an OD process can also inform the development of AI as a research approach.

Regarding AI research activity, researchers are faced with a number of questions about how they should carry out their studies, questions stimulated by the debates and discussions in the research methodologies discussed in this chapter. While each approach has its own sets of procedures that follow from the worldview espoused, AI can be seen to have links with many of these and therefore may need to develop an eclectic mix of approaches, not only to be true to the principles of focusing on success in order to facilitate change but also to be coherent and transparent. This is a tall order: to take on the thinking of these different methodologies in a way that demonstrates integrity and consistency. It will involve the issues that have been outlined here about worldview context and change, but it will also involve the issues of roles and relationships, with dimensions of power, knowledge, and skill. Embracing all of these issues fits with the work of Clandinin and

Huber (2002), who offered "a metaphor to help us represent the wholeness of our lives" (p. 163), a metaphor of three-dimensional exploration, first, of place *(context)*, second, of time *(change)*, and, third, of person. Thus, the next chapter discusses the dimension of how roles and relationships can be considered in AI research.

This returns the discussion to the founding concepts of AI. It was developed to be inclusive and collaborative and to focus on building on the positive. These concepts or themes present some challenges for research projects that wish to incorporate these ideas in an environment in which selection and control have been important aspects of inquiry. In addition, AI work takes place in real time, and the researcher may be a member of the community being studied or a researcher from another organization, and so the dimensions of chronology and positionality are also key aspects in conducting AI research. The next chapter focuses on these issues of how AI research plays out in practice.

4

Key Themes and Dimensions in AI Research

❖　❖　❖

The previous chapters have outlined the key features of Appreciative Inquiry (AI) as an organizational development (OD) strategy, the implications this has for developing a congruent research methodology, and research models that can be linked to AI. This has been a rather abstract overview, concerned with laying out the basic concepts and principles of AI in each of these methodological fields, with particular attention paid to the dimensions of place and time. In this chapter, these basic concepts are brought together by exploring the particular issues that arise for researchers using AI: the issues of roles and relationships that permeate all research stages and settings, which is the third dimension of "person" suggested by Clandinin and Huber (2002).

In this chapter, exploration is organized around the themes and dimensions that are evident in AI discussions and the issues of person and relationship that can become evident in carrying out AI research. The *themes*, as has been suggested, come from AI discussions in OD and research and are identified here as themes of inclusivity and a focus on the positive. The *dimensions* that are discussed in this chapter may present in research practice but may not be so fully explored in texts, similar to what Reinharz (1979) called the "experienced dimension" of research. Here, these dimensions are presented as being about, first, the chronology of the research, the way in which roles and relationships change over the course of a study; second, the position of the researcher as insider or outsider; and third, power, as different participants display and exercise different degrees and forms of control over the AI process. This type of organization is one way of presenting debates, though any form of demarcation tends to neglect the way in which issues also merge and blend with each other. When reading the following pages, then, it must remembered that links between ideas are as important as the way, in this chapter, they are treated separately.

❖ THEMES: INCLUSIVITY AND FOCUS ON THE POSITIVE

Two main themes are discussed in this chapter: first, themes of *inclusivity*, whereby the aim is that as many people as possible are involved in study in a collaborative way, and, second, the theme of *discovering the positive*, whereby the conversations and stories told are about achievements and successes. Both themes are evident in discussions of AI as an OD approach but also raise issues for AI as a research approach, running counter to some of the principles of other types of research. Crossing these themes are three main dimensions: first, the *chronology of the study*, or the sequence of research activities and choices; second, the *position of the researchers*, or whether they are part of the culture being studied (insiders) or have come to the world being studied simply and only to carry out the study (outsiders); and third, *power*, or the different types and processes of influence that participants may have.

Inclusivity

Inclusivity is a powerful theme in AI texts that focus on OD. Writers of OD texts that describe the process of AI argue that including as many people as possible in the AI activity can help to facilitate support for the process, so that knowledge, understanding, and participation are not confined to a small, elite group whose conclusions may be rejected by others who have not been involved in the AI work. Invitations to participate should be extended to all key players inside and outside groups and organizations, to include as many views and experiences as possible and to develop strategies that have a widespread resonance and acceptance.

The emphasis on inclusivity in OD has a clear rationale behind it: It facilitates OD by drawing on the experiences of as many people as possible, harnessing their energy and commitment. When this principle is transferred over to research methodology, however, a number of different questions can be raised. These questions, by and large, stem from the debates about *sampling,* or the choice of people to involve in a study, that are found in research methodology discussions, often about the extent to which the findings of one study of one sample can be *generalized* and applied to a wider population.

This view of sampling and generalization is usually found in quantitative research, where sample characteristics are matched against the characteristics of the population from which they are derived. The matching may require strategic approaches, such as *stratified sampling,* in which potential subjects are grouped according to characteristics of interest to the study, or *random sampling,* in which subjects have a random chance of selection (note the use of the term *subject* here, traditional in this form of research). Because the chance of selection can be calculated mathematically, the findings from the sample can be mathematically extrapolated to the wider population. As this description suggests, this form of sampling is driven by processes and calculations that enable a mathematical argument to be made that findings can be generalizable; in other words, examining the sample can tell you something about the members of the group who were not included in it.

In AI, this notion of sampling does not fit. Samples in AI are not usually randomly generated; rather, strategic decisions are made about whom to invite to take part in a study, depending on the experience, knowledge, and understanding the researcher thinks they might have. This comes closer to ideas in qualitative research, in which sampling is described as purposeful or theoretical. *Theoretical sampling* was discussed in some detail by Glaser and Strauss (1967), in their presentation of grounded theory, and referred to a process by which sampling was driven by reflection on emerging theory. An example would be a study of staff working in a shop that indicated that account-holding customers had a particular view of the shop and their relationships to it, and so theoretical sampling processes would be invoked to ensure that this theoretical idea was explored through the inclusion of account holders in the study.

The notion of theoretical sampling fits better with the idea of AI as a strategic activity, in which ideas are developed as the study progresses, but some caveats must be made. First, there is a question about the degree of control and choice the *researcher* (a term used here as shorthand for whoever is carrying out the study) has about the way in which people are invited to take part in an AI study—sometimes the group exercises control in the area, and the researcher has to go along with this. People who may be theoretically important in the researcher's eyes may not be important in the view of the rest of the group. Second, all forms of sampling have a tendency to avoid discussing the distinction between inviting participation and actually taking part. Invitations can be issued, but people might not accept, and in this case, the study has to go ahead with participants who have agreed to take part, and they might not be the participants who are wanted or needed.

These caveats point to one of the key features of AI as an OD and as a research approach, and that is the collaborative nature of the work. This means that choices about invitations are made collectively, not by individual researchers, and that agreement to take part can entail involvement that is more than just providing data; it also has to do with making decisions about how and what information or data are needed.

Some research models can provide frameworks for this inclusivity and the issues and questions that it raises. The development of ethnography, for example, has included a growing awareness of the complexity of social worlds and the need to explore this complexity in order to reach a comprehensive understanding of the researched world. Similarly, the principles of action research have pointed to the importance of involving a range of people in the process so that understanding and support for change can come from the people who will live with the consequences of the study, and this can help or hinder implementation. Further impetus to inclusivity is offered by the concepts of case study methodology, which stress the importance of identifying the dynamics and boundaries of the case and the implications of setting limits for the way that the case is defined and explored. Another model to add to the debate on inclusivity is that of critical theory, which argues that one of the purposes of research is to challenge accepted and taken-for-granted ideas. Following this, there is a strong argument that invitations to participate in an AI study should be made to people who have diverse positions and views, to increase opportunities to hear different voices and ideas.

These frameworks provide arguments for inclusivity that are linked to a range of different methodological positions. The idea of inclusivity, however, can be embraced in different degrees, from an inclusion of a limited range of participants in narrow roles (for example, as providers of information) to a wide range of participants in extensive roles (for example, planning and presenting research).

Paradoxically, the degree of inclusivity may be decided by the researcher or whoever starts the research process off. The paradox is, of course, that being able to decide the degree of inclusivity is in itself a privileged position. This points to inclusivity as covering researchers as well, because they are also a part of the process of exploration—studies are not something they do *to* others, but something they do *with* others. This has major implications for the way research is carried out. The following chapters explore this in some detail, as stages in research are discussed.

Extended involvement, in which participants are involved to a considerable degree or in large numbers, raises several questions, and those are issues of ownership and responsibility. In traditional research practice, there are many occasions when an individual researcher is accorded responsibility for a study. This might be as a budget holder for a study or as lead author of reports and papers; the main point is that it is customary to view one person as responsible for a study and having ownership of it, someone who can be called to account if things go wrong. Where there is extended inclusion and a number of people are participating in a study, this responsibility can become confused. Systems of financial accounting or copyright clearance, for example, operate in well-defined ways derived from legal frameworks, and these very rarely embrace informal agreements of shared responsibility. This discomfort can also apply to the way groups work on a less official level. If a participant feels that a study should go in a particular way, for example, by asking particular questions, an inclusive model of participation would suggest that this would be respected and acted on. What the model does not tease out, however, is what should happen if there are disagreements or differences.

This suggests that part of adopting an inclusive approach in AI research should be the thinking through of how differences can be managed, which may involve establishing some process of canvassing, presenting, and deciding between different views and ideas. This process needs to be agreed on and supported by participants, and negotiating this may involve establishing areas in which different participants have expertise and knowledge or finding out where it can be accessed.

The strengths and potential issues arising from different forms of involvement are summarized in Table 4.1.

There are very good reasons, therefore, for thinking through the implications of an inclusive approach to AI research. Such an approach echoes much of the pragmatic, ethical, and theoretical debates about research, particularly when there is an interest in supporting change

4.1   Implications of Involvement

Form of Involvement	Strengths	Issues
Extensive involvement—participants fully part of all study activity.	More support for ideas generated. More knowledge and experience available.	Differences and disagreements may be more evident, and decision-making process can be complex.
Limited involvement—participants part of limited aspects of the study.	More sustainable involvement in view of other commitments. More focused involvement.	Transience of participants may affect group dynamics. Contributions may be unrelated to progress of whole project.

(debates in action research in particular can inform thinking here). This may run into areas of debate and dispute, however, when different participants have differing views (and narrative methodology points to the way these differences can be manifest) or when the research group negotiates with external agencies who assume that models of individual responsibility are operating.

Focus on the Positive

A second theme in the literature on AI as an OD strategy is a focus on the positive, the idea of inquiry being *appreciative*. As seen in the second chapter, this interest in achievement has been advocated in AI as a useful way of moving practice on, starting from a process of building on "what works" rather than what is going wrong or failing. This is supported by a series of arguments or principles that point to the empowering ideas of appreciation: if people are supported in exploring success, these stories can empower them and they can carry forward ideas about achievement into their plans for the future. These plans may involve building on achievement to change practice or to reinforce it.

Although it can be seen that in OD, focusing on the positive would have a useful and challenging impact on people used to punitive fault-finding, there is difficulty in relating this idea to debates about research methodologies and the aim of developing a comprehensive understanding of a phenomenon. From this perspective, a focus on asking positive questions looks like a restricted approach: By excluding talk of the negative, only a partial account is produced.

While a positive focus can be justified in OD as a useful way of encouraging support for change in an organization, in research, it poses more problems. It can be justified on pragmatic grounds as being an approach that is more likely to encourage participants to provide information and talk about their experiences in a nonthreatening atmosphere. This pragmatic concern, however, does not reflect some theoretical concerns that might arise, that is, the idea of a partial account that ignores or neglects negative stories. A focus on the positive, then, can be seen as offering only a limited understanding of a phenomenon.

The notion of focusing on the positive, expressed in the principles of AI, gives the approach its unique and distinctive nature. Applying this notion to the development of research methodology, however, may not always be a straightforward matter. Much as early advocates of AI as an OD tool faced criticisms from those who had based strategies on the ideas of problem finding and problem solving, using AI as a research approach can present researchers with criticisms of selectivity or incomplete exploration. The idea that research should present a comprehensive picture, "warts and all," is a very powerful one, and it provides a basis for the claims of research to be impartial.

Looking at models of research, one can see that few frameworks are easily invoked to support a positive focus. Drivers for inclusivity are fairly easy to find, but these rationales are largely made on the basis of providing a comprehensive coverage of the researched world. Focusing on the positive, however, means being selective rather than inclusive, and so the models found in ethnography, for example, do not support this approach. Even the model that advocates engagement with the researched world, action research, seems, on first examination, to advocate a problem-solving approach, in other words, a focus on difficulties or barriers. Action research, however, does suggest some arguments about ensuring collaboration that can lend themselves to the case for AI. If the purpose of the research is not just to contribute to understanding, but to support change (as in action research), AI makes a strong case for supporting change through its focus on the positive. The principles of AI, including the poetic principle, the anticipatory principle, and the positive principle (discussed in Chapter 2), indicate that change is promoted through building on the positive rather than concentrating on problems. People are more likely to engage in thinking through and acting on change strategies if the process begins with a positive stance. Paradoxically, the ideas of critical theory may also be applied here. If people are used to thinking of themselves as being unsuccessful, using AI to ask questions about achievements can be a valuable way of challenging those ideas, allowing people to think more critically (that is, to take a more comprehensive view) about what they do and the circumstances in which they do it.

A number of other arguments can be made to support the emphasis on the positive in AI research. One is that all research is partial, in the sense that it always has a focus and area of interest and that exploring positive experiences should be thought of simply as a particular focus. A study of promotion procedures in an organization, for example, would not be expected to explore all areas of the organizational world, but to concentrate on features that are relevant to the research question. The study might, then, observe interviews, but would not be criticized if it did not investigate the menus in the canteen, unless, of course, an argument were made that they were important to understanding promotion.

The argument for a focus on the positive has credibility if the claims made for the study are equally focused and related to other studies in the field. If the study claimed to be a definitive study of a phenomenon—complete and extensive—this claim would be difficult to sustain. A researcher can, however, say that the study needs to be read as part of a body of work, the collection of studies done on the topic, which will have asked different questions and used different approaches. The AI study is, therefore, one study among others, part of an approach to redressing the balance in the body of work, which, if it is in line with traditional research approaches, will have primarily explored problems and deficits (perhaps along with positive aspects). The idea of seeing a study as part of a body of work moves away from the image of research as being a disengaged and distinct exercise, carried out in isolation from all other conversations, and therefore sheds a different light on issues such as validity and knowledge. While the study can and should be assessed as a distinct activity, its contribution to the collective effort in the field also needs to be examined. No one study can claim to do everything, and an AI study should be clear about its aims and the extent to which it achieves them—an exploration of the positive. This is not to advocate a cozy mutual appreciation between researchers, who need to progress knowledge through debate and challenge, but an awareness that research studies do not stand in isolation from each other.

The implications of a positive focus are outlined in Table 4.2.

This focus on the positive also has some general implications for the way that research is conducted. It has been pointed out that many

Table 4.2   Strengths and Challenges of a Positive Focus

Strengths	Challenges
Can redress emphasis on problems, contributing to a body of knowledge.	Can present a partial rather than a comprehensive picture.
Can promote support and participation by promoting reflection on achievements.	Can seem to avoid difficulties and challenges.

people's experiences of research (and of OD) may have been negative experiences in which the discussion addressed the people's problems. An AI study, then, may be an unexpected process, with participants being puzzled or suspicious. These possible responses suggest that AI work needs to be sustained over time, so that people can review and reflect on their initial ideas about AI, and this work needs to be open and collaborative. This relates the points made above, about inclusivity, in which the arguments arose from the idea that including different people and different views would lead to a richer picture of the world if they were involved in the study in a collaborative way. This point also applies to the idea of positive focus: AI work needs to be sustained over time in order to give people time to get used to the different approach used, and if the work is sustained over time, this will also involve collaboration, as people will not stay around for something they have no stake in.

❖ DIMENSIONS: PROJECT CHRONOLOGY, RESEARCHER POSITIONS, AND POWER AND CONTROL

In addition to the broad themes of inclusivity and a focus on the positive, more particular dimensions need to be acknowledged in AI studies, involving the shared experiences of the people involved or participating in a study. These are, first, the temporal dimensions of project chronology—the stage of the project and the activities that this may involve; second, the personal position of the researcher as internal or external to the group of people being researched, the people I have called research "participants"; and third, issues of power and control. These dimensions stretch across studies, shaping activity, relationships, and processes.

Chronology

Chronology was discussed in the last chapter, relating to the way that some research methodologies incorporate an interest in developments over time. The discussion here is more practical, in that it focuses on the immediate concerns of the ways in which people may carry out different activities at different stages of a project. Stages of a project are often thought of and described in discrete and linear terms, particularly when writing a proposal or a report, which might identify stages such as proposing and planning a study, carrying it out, and reporting on it. While this model does seem a little too neat and tidy, with clear markers between stages that may not be so distinct in "real life," it does have the advantage of highlighting the chronology of a study as it moves through periods in which different issues of roles and relationships come to the fore. The movement might be meandering rather than linear, and phases may be blurred rather than clear, but a chronological framework does draw attention to ideas of change and development within a study.

In the initial phase of developing a proposal, the key issue for researchers will likely have to do with identifying useful questions from an AI perspective and ways in which they might be answered. These questions will be about exploring the positive, and the methods of answering them will be based on understanding and knowledge of the ways in which participants talk together. In the phase of conducting the study, the overall goals and ideas about methods still apply, but there may be practical issues that become apparent only when the study gets under way. In the phase of drawing conclusions and telling others about the study, the issue of questions also informs debates on the issues of audience, language, and interests that come to the fore. Throughout the study, then, issues do not simply arise, get solved, and then disappear; they occupy shifting positions, moving from immediate and pressing debates to background and lower-profile questions, and back again. The key issues at different stages of AI studies are discussed in more detail in the following chapters, but here, the general point is that projects have a chronology and this centers around the ideas that participants and audiences have about the development of the study. This chronology can be lost or forgotten in the business of decision making, but this loss can decontextualize activity: Forgetting the past or the future can make the present seem puzzling.

Chronology: Sequence

Awareness of a chronological dimension to a study points to some implications that need thinking through. First, there is the implication that study activities will take place in sequence, so that they will follow from and lead to each other. In research manuals, these sequences are fairly uniform: There is a planning stage, a sampling stage, a data collection stage, analysis, and, finally, dissemination stages. This tradition has a logical flow to it. Data cannot be analyzed until they are collected, and they cannot be collected before some decisions are made about how to collect them.

This sequence does reflect the way some studies are carried out and, importantly, the way some people think studies ought to be carried out. Following this sequence can be seen as meeting the criteria of purposeful research that has a clear aim (for example, a hypothesis to test). This aim would have been indicated by a review of the literature that showed gaps in knowledge that needed to be filled or anomalies that needed to be clarified. Because the aims are so precisely defined, the methodology is a logical consequence: It is clear what the sample should be, what data should be collected, and what data analysis should take place. This, however, is an ideal version of research, and there are many points at which this design can be modified: Previous research may not produce clear questions; samples may not be accessible; data may not be collectable; and data analysis may not be as extensive as first hoped. At each of these points, researchers may indicate the difficulties they have had and the alternatives they have chosen. These changes, however, are often portrayed as compromises and deviations, rather than sensible and creative responses to the complexities of the researched world. This rather disparaging view of methodological choices may also be held by readers and reviewers of the research.

At the other end of the sequencing spectrum is the study in which nothing is decided in advance and stages follow each other in unpredictable ways. This type of study can be viewed as following the model offered by ethnographic studies, in which questions are broad and sources of data uncertain until the study gets under way. Here, sampling might be theoretical, such that participants are identified as areas of theoretical interest to be developed, and data collection methods may be chosen as the researcher learns more about the acceptability and utility of different tools. The criteria for sequencing may center around the way in which studies have been responsive to the researched world and less restricted by predetermined plans. Hence, stages may be repeated or revisited or may be blurred and developed creatively. One example can be seen in the stages of sampling and data collection, which in the predetermined study might follow each other but in the responsive study may be cycles, such that the next stage of data collection follows from the previous one. This process may follow directions that were not anticipated when the study began, including revisiting some stages.

The two models, the *predetermined* and the *responsive* sequences, are, of course, extreme models and are very rarely found in these "pure" forms. Responsive research is probably more planned and predetermined research more open than at first seems. AI research comes somewhere between these two positions. Because of its interest in exploring the previously unexplored, it needs to be responsive to the particular settings and contexts in which it takes place—they cannot be predetermined. At the same time, however, the focus is on exploring a particular area of life—what works well—and this focus will entail some preplanning and thought. AI research, then, is neither a completely unstructured process of seeing what happens nor is it planned with precision prior to data collection.

The notion of sequencing, then, may play out in different ways in each AI study, and the criteria used for both preplanned and responsive studies may not fit. AI researchers may need to be able to argue a case for inductive study development, as ideas and opportunities for data collection present themselves as the study progresses, and also a case for a focus on what is going well in the setting, following from the rationale behind AI and a specific interest in the issue that has triggered the study.

Chronology: Pacing

A second aspect of study chronology is the pacing of activity. With some studies, it may be relatively easy to map out the time each activity is likely to take up. Interviews, for example, might be estimated to take 1 hour to conduct, and if participants are easily available, this can be drawn up as a quite detailed schedule. In AI studies, however, carrying out a study is likely to be complex, with processes of engagement in the study affected by many different factors. These will include the various responsibilities and commitments that participants already have and will continue to have beyond the study. In accounts of AI as an OD strategy, it is sometimes indicated that these commitments have been put to one side as the organization devotes energy to the AI work. When AI takes place as a research activity, this organizational support might not be so strongly evident, and as a consequence, other activities may be prioritized over the AI work. This makes estimating availability of participants and the duration of their involvement more difficult to plan.

Before the AI study starts, however, there are processes of learning and debate that have to be engaged in, and the speed at which they progress will determine how and when the AI study can begin (although in many ways, this discussion can be seen as part of AI work). Previously, it was mentioned that AI is very different from other approaches in its approach to exploration, both in research or OD. This may make it difficult for participants to place AI in the context of other approaches they have come across, and this may slow down or speed up a study in a number of ways. Participants may feel so enthusiastic that they carry out activities quickly, or they may feel suspicious and delay or divert activity. Progress may be variable, as participants go through different phases of enthusiasm and concern, and made more difficult to predict when participants work with people who have not been part of the central discussions and debates. In a study in which participants interview other people, for example, this process may be governed by the views of the participants and the views of the people they interview.

The pacing of an AI study may, therefore, be difficult to predict, and when the complexities of sequencing, discussed above, are added, it can be difficult to anticipate how a study may progress. Some of the activities affecting the pace of a study are laid out in Table 4.3.

While the "Stage of Study" column in Table 4.3 does look overly demarcated, it does at least give some sense of sequence, which, even at such a broad level of description, identifies the different activities these stages may involve. Returning to these activities, however, it can

Table 4.3   Stages of a Study and Main Activities

Stage of Study	Activity
Starting a study	Discussing and debating AI goals. Developing support and collaborative working processes. Planning and exploring data collection strategies.
Carrying out a study	Maintaining, reviewing, and reflecting on processes and progress. Identifying data sources. Collecting data.
Ending a study	Coming to conclusions. Outlining consequences. Identifying audiences. Presenting and writing reports and papers.

be seen that they are even more difficult to put boundaries and timelines around. Many of them are interpersonal tasks, about discussing issues with participants, and the time they will take is difficult to specify, particularly when it is realized that they will be revisited and repeated throughout the study—there is no clear episodic structure in which activities have a clear beginning and ending. The interpersonal element of AI, then, makes study chronology difficult to pin down beyond broadly identifying that different stages involve different activities and that priorities for these activities may change as the study progresses.

Researcher Position

The second dimension outlined here is the issue of researcher position, here focusing on whether the researcher (or researchers) is an "insider/actor" or "outsider/observer" in relation to the group of participants. This is a more fluid dimension than first appears, as researchers occupy shifting and ambiguous positions throughout a study (Reed & Procter, 1994). To summarize, the researcher position is a reflection of membership, alliance, and interest and shapes a number of ways in which the study takes place. As Bobasi, Jackson, and Wilkes (2005) argued,

Clearly, the theoretical position that underpins the use of self as instrument for data collection has implications for how one might represent a world or adapt a methodology. This is so because the position adopted by a researcher in the field affects every phase of the research process, from the way the research question/problem is initially constructed, designed and conducted to the ways in which reports and publications arising from the study are presented. (p. 495)

Bobasi et al. further argued that "the recent proliferation of publications devoted to the self in qualitative work is indicative of its perceived significance" (p. 494). (Coffey, 1999, and Willis, 2000, are examples of this interest.) They went on to critique those who have maintained traditional views of the researcher position:

Notwithstanding the increasing recognition of the role of self in the collection, analysis and interpretation of data, there are critics who argue that some ethnographies continue to represent culture through a "tell it like it is" approach. It is as if there were only one reality, even if they recognize that reality is influenced by the researcher and vice versa. (Bobasi et al., 2005, p. 495)

If the researcher is seen as an insider, that is, part of the culture being studied (for example, an existing member of staff takes on a research role), this creates particular research dynamics. These may include familiarity with the context, which makes negotiating collaboration easier but may also require reexamination to avoid "taking the world for granted," or not being critically aware of what seems everyday and unremarkable. As part of the world being studied, the researchers play out roles that go beyond the focus of the study. They will have developed responsibilities and roles that preceded the study and will endure after it finishes. Similarly, if the researcher is an outsider (brought into the organization specifically to work on the study), this is a particular position that needs to be taken into account. He or she may approach the setting as a "strange" world, and this unfamiliarity may entail a process of learning, which may be complex and lengthy. On the other hand, this "naïveté" may allow the outsider researcher to ask questions and propose views that would not be voiced by someone who was accustomed to the world being studied.

The insider position is, perhaps, a less common one, as traditional divisions between research and practice have fostered situations in which outsider researchers are called in as "experts" to examine activity. The outsider's distance is seen as advantageous in many ways, not least because they are viewed as being unaffected by local interests and therefore more able to be objective about what they observe. They may be affected by the politics of the academic world, but not by the researched world. The insider researcher position, however, is a relatively new phenomenon and has been regarded with suspicion as having too many interests tied up with the researched world, such as working relationships, promotion prospects, or workplace facilities, to be able to stand back from the data (Reed & Procter, 1994). While the insider researcher may have a long-standing knowledge and experience of the researched world, which makes learning quicker than it would be for an outsider, this knowledge may need to be critically reviewed to identify assumptions and expectations that may shape research activity in far-reaching ways.

Both positions place the relationships between the researcher and other participants in particular contexts. These are likely to be unique to each situation, with a mix of different processes. For the insider researcher, the transition to project leader may be a change of role and function that is smooth or difficult, and for the outsider, the process of

Table 4.4   Characteristics of Researcher Position, as Insider/Actor or
            Outsider/Observer

	Insider/Actor	Outsider/Observer
Entry	Already there.	Introduced.
Stay	Constant reiteration of research role.	Constant reflection on learning and experience of setting.
Exit	Does not happen as part of the study.	Expected/planned.

becoming part of the group for the study may be welcomed or be a cause for concern. It is not that one position is advantageous and the other is not or that for each position, there are better or worse ways of managing relationships; it is simply that these positions are important to acknowledge and be aware of. This is important in any study, whatever the methodology, but in AI research, with dimensions of inclusivity and a focus on building on the positive, positionality is brought into sharper focus. Inclusivity and an exploration of the positive are interpersonal dimensions, not simply technical procedures, and the way in which the researcher and fellow participants see positionality shapes the way in which they are played out.

The characteristics of researcher position are summarized in Table 4.4, which sets out differences between insiders and outsiders at different stages of a study.

Positionality can shape the development of collaborative research in a number of ways. For an insider researcher, preexisting relationships and roles may direct the way participants work together: Previous alliances and disagreements may make collaboration more or less possible or introduce dynamics that contribute toward the way collaboration works. For an outsider, similar processes apply. An outsider may be regarded with suspicion or welcomed as someone who has a new perspective, and whatever these ideas are, they will go toward the development of particular collaborative relationships, wary or open, suspicious or enthusiastic, or a mix of all of these.

As Bobasi et al. (2005) argued,

In other words, researchers should account for self in the field [here, they refer to Altheide & Johnson, 1994] and be aware of and be able to justify how their own positions and interests are imposed at all stages of the research process—from the questions they ask, to those they choose to ignore, from whom they study to whom they ignore, from problem-formation to analysis, representation and writing [here, they refer to Hertz, 1996]. (p. 495)

Power and Control

The themes of inclusivity and positive focus and the dimensions of chronology and researcher position are issues that shape and frame efforts to combine and apply the ideas that have developed from the discussions of AI both as an OD approach and as a research methodology. In addition, there is the overarching dimension of power and control: Who directs the way a study progresses? Throughout this book, there has been discussion of collaboration and how it is vital for AI work, reflecting the themes of inclusivity and positive focus, and how it can be shaped by the dimensions of chronology and positionality. The development of collaboration, however, is a process that involves thinking about issues of power and control. In some ways, the idea of power and control does not sit easily in a social constructionist framework, which suggests that the world is, at least in part, a product of our thinking: We construct features of our lives, a point discussed in the previous chapter. Power is a concept that cannot go unadressed. It is to be seen not as something that exists in the same way a dimension of the physical world does, but as something that we collectively construct. In this understanding of power, it is something that we collectively make and respond to: No one can exercise power without the collaboration of others.

Having said this, however, it seems to be an enduring feature of social life that power and control are exercised, whether by a process of co-construction or not, and that power is a real issue that affects the way we live. Dismissing power as a product of our thoughts and feelings, with little effect on the way we live our lives, is a position that neglects the way that it affects what we do.

This is displayed in three areas of research. First, power can affect the way a group or organization calls for or initiates research; second, it can affect the way groups work together; and, third, it can affect the way research is responded to. These three areas are, of course, interrelated, but they can usefully be discussed separately as part of the process of identifying ways in which power and control can be exercised. These are laid out in Table 4.5.

From Table 4.5, it can be seen that each of the arenas involves a range of activities that can be debated and disputed. Many of these

Table 4.5   Research Areas and Questions About Power and Control

Area	Activities
Initiating research	Suggesting questions: Are they approved or resisted?
	Deciding research questions: Are they negotiated or imposed?
	Establishing roles and relationships: Are they agreed or disputed?
Working together	Public scrutiny of stages and plans: Are comments responded to?
	Negotiating consent with participants: Is this a transparent or obscure process?
	Collecting data: Is this idiosyncratic or coordinated?
Responding to research	Authorship: shared or individual?
	Conclusions: agreed or disputed?
	Presentations: collective or separate?
	Rationalizing methodology: shared understanding or different views?
	Usefulness: seen by all?

disputes will involve an exercise of power, depending on the status and control of resources that participants have. This may vary across arenas; participants who work in administration may have more power over research reports, for example, because they direct the resources for typing and reprographics. For different aspects of the study, then, there may be different dynamics operating. Elements can be directed by the researcher, whose decisions and choices are followed, developed in partnership across all participants through a process of discussion, and led by participants whose views take priority. These different dynamics of power and control are summarized in Table 4.6, along with some of the issues that may accompany them.

Bobasi et al. (2005) pointed to the way that some researchers have been aware of power differences and taken steps to redress this imbalance: "Although there is acknowledgement that the relationship between researcher and participant inherently involves power differentials, feminist researchers adopt strategies to minimize power inequities as far as possible" (p. 495). Examples of such strategies include constructing the encounter as an information exchange (a two-way movement of information), rather than just a data collection

Table 4.6   Dynamics of Power and Control

Dynamic	Issues
Directed by researcher	May have an academic focus and speak to an audience of academic colleagues rather than addressing practice concerns. Familiar with and has access to academic resources and facilities, such as research publications and funding bodies.
Partnership	Can be difficult to maintain and establish without attention to collaborative processes.
Led by participants	May be driven by immediate practice concerns rather than wider issues of knowledge development. Familiar with and has access to organizational resources and facilities, such as staff lists, services, and premise.

exercise (which implies a one-way movement of information), and giving space for participant concerns to be raised. Echoing these ideas, similar strategies may be useful for AI research when power differences threaten studies.

❖ CONCLUSION

This chapter has outlined some of the complexities of integrating the worlds of OD and research and some of the factors AI researchers may have to negotiate. These factors are complex and may be unique to each context, but an attempt has been made to identify key issues and the way that the themes of inclusivity and positive focus and the dimensions of chronology, positionality, and power interact.

Some of the complexities of the way these factors play out are suggested in Table 4.7.

These complexities are partly shaped by the differences among and between participants. While it is tempting to think of them as a homogenous group, they may have different aims when participating in studies, and these are outlined in Table 4.8.

These are just some of the possibilities, and even in this limited list, there are obvious potential differences. The complexity is added to

Table 4.7   Research Stage, Position, and Power and Developing Inclusivity and Positive Focus

	Project Stage: Beginning	Project Stage: Concluding	Researcher Position: Insider	Researcher Position: Outsider	Powerful Participant	Powerless Participant
Inclusivity	Extending invitations	Marking endings	Changing relationships	Beginning relationships	Deciding who is invited	Accepting who is invited
Focus on the positive	Introducing new ideas	Confirming and building on ideas	Starting with prior experiences of the context	Starting with unfamiliarity	Decides how *positive* is defined	Accepts how *positive* is defined

Table 4.8   Different Research Goals and Expectations for Different Participants

Participants	Possible Goals
Coresearchers	To develop expertise and understanding of research
Users/customers	To improve the quality/availability/value of what they get from the organization
Providers/workers	To improve the quality of the organizational experience

when considering that people's roles change. They may, for example, be providers of one facility and users of another and, overlaying this, may have a third role as coresearchers. In addition, there are a number of other players outside the research group: the possible audiences for the study. These audiences can be forgotten, as they stand some distance away from the immediate concerns of the researchers, but their influence should not be underestimated. Some audiences and concerns are shown in Table 4.9 and discussed in more depth in the next chapter, in which the planning of AI studies is related to the different interests that potential supporters may have.

When organizing an AI study, there are a number of factors to take into account in order to facilitate an inclusive and positive study that is supported throughout the study by a range of participants and audiences. This means more than just taking the principles of AI as an OD strategy and applying them within a research framework. There are differences between OD and research, and these differences have to do with the criteria used in each for validity. What is a straightforward matter to justify as an OD tool needs to meet different criteria in the world of research. The criteria go beyond looking at the results or findings of a study; they include rationales and descriptions of the process of data collection, through all of the choices made about who to involve, what data to collect, and how the information can be analyzed. This chapter has tried to lay out some of the complexities and issues that will shape researchers' decisions, including links that can be made to the OD literature and the research methodology literature. It is clear that every study will face different issues, and different decisions will be made in each one, and so this chapter has not provided instructions to follow, but simply posed questions and pointed to

Table 4.9   Potential Research Audiences and Concerns

Audience	Concern
Funders	Does this represent value for money?
Coresearchers	Does this respond to my ideas and concerns?
Academic referees	Does this meet academic criteria for good research?
Practitioners	Does this address useful questions for my practice?
Users/customers	Does this lead to improvements in services?

important issues. The rest of this book goes on to look at different stages of research and how these may play out, and this chapter is a foundation for these debates, setting out the key issues and questions for researchers.

5

Developing Research Questions and Goals With Communities

A key feature of Appreciative Inquiry (AI), as seen in previous chapters, is that it involves the partnership and participation of a range of people who come together to explore their world. This idea of collaboration or inclusivity also shapes the way AI research is planned and proposed, and it resonates with ideas of "relational responsibility" set out by McNamee and Gergen (1999). Here, the move is away from thinking about phenomena as being explainable by individual ideas and actions, but, instead, as being understandable by the perspectives brought to bear by and communicated by people in webs of relationships. Similarly, developing AI research ideas is not something individuals do in isolation from everyone else, but something they do with others.

The process of developing AI research ideas may involve encouraging participation, support, approval, or funding, and it may make the difference between being able to do the research or not, or at least making the process easier. Participation and support are essential in AI research if it is to reflect an ethos of inclusivity. Funding is clearly important for some studies that will need resources to carry out the research; approval may be needed to obtain permission to do the study in the form that has been chosen (for example, a student needs permission to register for a research-based course); and all input is welcome, to provide opportunities for discussion, encouragement, and reflection. Developing and presenting an AI research plan, however, may meet with a mixed response from people who are not familiar with the approach or are wary of it.

One important tension seems to lie with people's ideas of what "good" research is. This was touched on in the first chapter of this book about initial AI experiences and followed up in the third chapter about methodology. Some of these ideas may come from traditional models of experimental or survey design. A part of the criteria by which these designs are judged is the extent to which they can demonstrate "objectivity," and this can be seen as the extent to which there is no bias in involvement; that is, every member of the population has an equal or measurable chance of being included, and questions asked are wide-ranging, encompassing both positive and negative elements. A trial of a health care treatment, for example, will collect data on unwanted side effects as well as beneficial effects; otherwise, researchers will be accused of bias or partial reporting.

These criteria for research are generally considered to be not just the criteria that a particular type of research should try to match, but that all studies should meet if they are to be "proper science." This view may be held by funding committees, the reviewers they call in to look at plans, colleagues who may be involved in a study, and the general public and press who might comment on research decisions. The criteria might be particularly important for funding bodies that have a concern about their public images, for example, those who are dependent on public donations to keep research going. The suggestion that some of the research they fund is not "good" science, then, can be a great concern for funders, who are not necessarily in the business of breaking academic barriers or taking a radical approach to research— they simply want to be confidant that what they fund is going to be sound according to the current criteria in use. Other audiences may have related ideas and concerns about supporting a study that may have reduced impact if its design is regarded as weak or flawed according to prevalent ideas about the characteristics of good research.

When an AI plan is presented, then, it can look to some as if it won't fit these characteristics. First, the people who will be invited to take part in the study will not be randomly selected, but will be identified because they are involved in a particular practice or organization that is the concern of the study. This can make the study appear "biased," as can the way in which the study is designed. A focus on appreciative questions, for example, which have an explicit interest in exploring "what works," will seem to be very selective and likely to explore only part of the phenomenon. If support is sought from the organization in which the study will take place, this approach may be more comfortable for the organization and less punitive than other investigations, but there may also be a concern that the organization may be seen as supporting only studies that will tell them they are doing well.

The second issue arises when an AI plan asks for support for things that are not usually part of traditional proposals. For example, to put ideas of inclusivity into practice, a plan may request funding for staff time or research partners to be involved in data collection or other activities usually done by a research assistant in a traditional academic environment. For some, this may breach rules on funding in which salary costs for people not employed solely by the project cannot be paid for. Sometimes, researchers may want to request funding for meetings, including travel, catering, and accommodation. Again, this might be against the rules for funding or simply a request that seems unusual or suspect.

Potential funders' concerns can also be shared by others who are presented with an AI research plan. Those responsible for approving students' proposals, for example, may use traditional criteria for "good" research, particularly in an academic world in which the way programs are developed and assessed may rest on long-established criteria based on ideas of individual ability rather than collective effort. These criteria may require research to be individual rather than collective work in order to assess the skills and attributes of the individual student, and so the involvement of a wider team may be thought to compromise the integrity of the study.

Some of these issues have come to the fore in work with students, in undergraduate or postgraduate programs, who have wanted to adopt an AI approach. While the case of a student might be seen as outside the mainstream of research, looking at the challenges that this situation presents can tell us something about the ideas of "good" science that are reflected in academic criteria for examination and evaluation of students.

In addition to the problems discussed above, there are problems in how an AI study fits with the purpose of a research project leading to an examination for an academic award. Examinations rely on traditional academic criteria according to which the student is required to demonstrate research competence. This means that a student may be expected to work individually rather than collaboratively, so that it is clear which is the student's work. Similarly, the student may be expected, or feel that he or she is expected, to have the design planned out in advance, and the discussion of this design is a way in which the student can demonstrate understanding of research methods. This is particularly the case when students are required to submit proposals rather than just final reports. Proposals are one way of seeing how much the student has understood. When a proposal is for an AI study, however, the study will involve a reflective and responsive approach, in which tools and strategies are developed as the study progresses, on the basis of emerging ideas, rather than being carefully planned in detail before the study begins.

In academic programs, it is also usual to require discussion of theoretical models, drawn from the core discipline of the program. As AI may have more pragmatic concerns, relevant theory may not always be at hand, and if the student's performance is assessed by his or her ability to think abstractly, discussion of practical issues may cause problems. Theory and practice are beginning to be seen as integrated rather than separate (this debate is returned to in the last chapter of this book), but traditions of discussing theory may use language and frameworks to embrace practices that have not yet developed and that remain esoteric in their presentation.

These three points, individual working, preplanned design, and abstract theory, are sometimes difficult to fit with some of the principles of AI: collaboration, responsive design, and practical application. It not surprising, then, that students can have difficulty meeting the criteria for examination. What they do have, though, is the opportunity to explore these difficulties at various points in the program, such as in essays and presentations, but there may still be times when they (and their supervisors) wish they had tackled something less complex.

People who may be presented less formally with an AI research plan, for example, colleagues, are not unaffected by the debates on definitions of "good research." For us, carrying out informal AI studies that have not needed approval or funding body review has still not been entirely smooth, because of the responses of colleagues with whom we have discussed our research. Sometimes these responses seem to reflect a world-weary suspicion of the term *Appreciative Inquiry*, which can seem like the latest trend in a field that is full of trends. As different camps in research make claims about the rigor of their approaches and the deficits of others, a competitive ethos is created, such that one way of doing research seeks to "win" by being "better" than the others. This has led to a situation in which one methodology becomes popular for a time but, almost inevitably, loses prominence as others take over. This can make AI seem like yet another "buzzword" that will pass in time. In these circumstances, getting intrigued or enthusiastic about AI seems like a waste of energy.

Other responses have owed something to an allegiance to traditional research approaches, in which AI can seem like an "unscientific" approach that is biased, chaotic, and opportunistic. Advice may be about ways to "tighten up" the study in ways that reflect these allegiances, but it can also undermine the researcher's confidence in the AI approach. The questions that are central to an AI approach, for example, may seem incomplete or partial to others, who may suggest other questions to "balance out" the study—these are usually questions that are unappreciative. Similarly, the open-ended aspects of an AI plan, in which the researcher intends to stay open to opportunities for data collection, can seem very disorganized and undisciplined in contrast to more detailed and definitive plans. Advice to make research design more structured and less flexible, then, can undermine some of the distinct qualities of AI, such as inclusivity and responsiveness.

❖ TALKING IN DIFFERENT COMMUNITIES

An initial stage of research is the development of research questions and aims, in other words, the refining of what may be general curiosity about contexts and activities to a more specific focus. The AI researcher may start off with the broad question "What's going on here that can be appreciated?" and then narrow this down to "How does this specific aspect take place?" This "narrowing comes" about partly because it is easier to focus on a particular dimension of a situation if the energies of the researcher are concentrated around a particular issue; and the traditional processes of developing a study, which include reviewing the literature and, from this, developing questions and deciding on methods and design, center on this "narrowing down." This process, however, is not always shaped entirely by the researchers—there are a number of different stakeholders with interests too, and if the researcher is to make the research useful, this needs to be thought through.

One way of thinking about this is to move away from the idea of research as an individual and private activity, in which it is seen as a demonstration of the unique brilliance of the single researcher or team, toward an idea of the research as being a collective activity, in which people share and develop ideas together. This idea invokes the image of a community of people working together to explore issues, and thinking about the different possibilities of goals and processes that this produces is one way of taking a fresh approach to research. To invoke the statement attributed to Diogenes, the Greek cynic philosopher, when anyone asked him where he came from, "I am a citizen of the world" (see Nussbaum, 2002, for a discussion of this). Similarly, one way of looking at research is to see it as having permeable, rather than impermeable, territorial boundaries, encouraging an inclusive and responsive process.

The notion of community, then, is not one that sets up limits, but points to possibilities of sharing and widening the focus from the individual researcher to others with interests and stakes. Reason (Reason & Bradbury, 2001), for example, talked about "communities of inquiry" as a central concern of action research, indeed, that "action research is only possible *with, for* and *by* persons and communities" (p. 2). Similarly, AI has to engage with a wider world than simply that of research if it is to support any change and development. Cooperrider and Whitney (1999) argued that this relational work is crucial in AI work of all kinds, and Anderson (1999) argued that this comes about through dialogue and discussion, with Tomm (1999) describing this as a process of "co-construction," as people get together to build ideas of joint action. This process moves away from traditional notions of authority to an idea of people working together to develop ideas of change (Friere, 1999). In the case of AI research, then, the ideas of working together in a collaborative way come together to shape the ways in which a dialogue can happen to plan the exploration of achievements.

The membership of a community is complex and multilayered. Communities may have a broad set of shared experiences and goals, but they may also have a range of different perspectives and aims. In addition to the complexity of each single community, the researcher may find there are a number of different communities with stakes in a research study. Researchers may, therefore, need to think through the dynamics of being connected to multiple and complex communities, so that they can anticipate and respond to the possibilities of the stance taken by other members. The next sections explore the complexities of being part of three communities, those of colleagues, of peers, and of customers (there may well be others that readers can think of). Each community is discussed in terms of their potential members, so that readers can think about links with them and possible interests and goals they may have. The way AI can be used within each community is then suggested, in the way that AI can address some of these perspectives and make contributions to the debates that communities are having. From this, a number of issues that cross communities are outlined, about roles and relationships, and then the diversity of goals and criteria for positive outcomes are explored. The chapter concludes by drawing out the implications of these issues for planning an AI study.

❖ COMMUNITY OF COLLEAGUES

The most obvious community researchers may belong to is the community of their *colleagues*—the people they work with. These are fellow practitioners, and the practice may be research, service delivery, or any other kind of activity. This shared experience gives colleagues a common perspective: the aims and goals of practice, the way these are evaluated, and the language that is used to discuss and describe them.

These "insider" conversations can allow several things to happen. They allow ideas to be shared and generated from everyday experiences of practice, and this can include questions, speculations, and hunches about the world of practice and about ways to study it. As a community of colleagues, members will have come across puzzles in their practice, instances of unexpected or unexplained events, which they feel the need to better understand. They may have had experiences of people talking about research that, in their view, has asked the wrong questions or used the wrong data in the wrong way and produced findings that are at best unusable, and at worst dangerous.

The example in Box 5.1 illustrates some of these points.

Box 5.1   Learning About Everyday Practice

During some exploratory observation in a long-term care ward for older people, I heard some exchanges between staff and service users that I found puzzling.

An exchange would take place in which a service user would swear and curse at a staff member, for example, asking where his or her (expletive!) lunch was. The member of staff would answer back, telling the older person about his or her meal, using similar language. The exchange would not sound threatening—indeed, it sounded relaxed and affectionate—but I decided to ask about this practice.

When I asked about this language, I was met by uncomprehending stares—nobody seemed to have thought that the use of such casual and

(Continued)

(Continued)

colloquial language would seem strange to a listener. When I pursued this and the realization dawned on them, both staff members and service users looked at me as if I was very stupid (I was, after all, a practitioner myself, and therefore, in their minds, part of the interaction and the vocabulary). They pointed out that this was everyday language, informal and friendly, and that it was appropriate to be used between people who had known each other a long time and felt comfortable with each other. As one service user said, "We don't stand on ceremony here—you'll have to get used to it!"

There were, of course, a number of issues that could be pursued here, for example, how interaction took place when people were not comfortable with swearing. These questions were, however, more about the way relationships developed, rather than applying some idea of what was a "correct" or "incorrect" form of communication.

Being a practitioner myself and aware of some ideas about relationships, much of this conversation made sense to me in the context of the care ward. It did not make much sense, however, to my supervisors, who heard my accounts. They interpreted the accounts as examples of conflict and possibly abuse, and expressed concern about my observations.

This example suggests that being a member of community in the care ward had made a number of things possible. First, because I was a familiar face, people had not "stood on ceremony," which meant that I had been able to hear things that outsiders might not have heard. Second, the explanation given to me by both staff members and service users had made sense to me, and I had been able to connect this with other experiences. Third, I had been able to imagine a set of questions that I could ask that would build on my observations and develop into an understanding of the ways in which older people and staff developed relationships, building on the skills they had developed. My membership of the community had meant that I had been aware of potential concerns for service users but had also understood the point of view offered by the care ward practitioners.

As the example in Box 5.1 suggests, being part of a community of colleagues can facilitate the development of questions, but it may also create problems. It may be difficult, for example, to be critical or challenge ideas in case doing this may have interpersonal consequences. For an "outsider," making challenges may be easier, as their time with participants is shorter and expected to end (Reed & Procter, 1994). This allows outsiders to feel that if any tension results from their questioning, they can escape it relatively easily, whereas colleagues may be with each other for some time and disagreements cannot be resolved so simply. This may lead to an environment in which conflict is avoided and mutual congratulation is preferred, which may not be the most useful way to explore practice. Sometimes, therefore, challenging questions to colleagues can be useful.

Another issue may be the insularity of the colleague community as debate and discussion become more focused on ideas and interactions among people who know each other and have shared the same experiences. There may be some reluctance to engage in debate with people from other places, particularly if the outside world is seen as hostile or critical. My experience of puzzlement when I asked about aspects of practice that colleagues felt I should have understood was a disincentive to further exploration—I could tolerate being thought of as stupid or naive for only limited periods of time. As this naïveté can be emphasized and valued in methodological discussions, I ran the risk of feeling inadequate either as a practitioner if I asked questions or as a researcher if I didn't.

Using AI can be a way of both respecting and expanding a community in the way it allows colleagues to describe their achievements in a nonthreatening and noncompetitive environment. By respecting the work that colleagues have done, it may become more possible to expand debates to look at what people in other places are doing and to identify ways this could inform and shape the work of colleagues. This can be a daunting prospect in environments marked by competitive relationships, in which defenses are clung to and the sharing of learning is a risky prospect. Using AI, however, can move these ideas on: Starting from the exploration of achievements places groups in a position in which more open discussion becomes more possible and practice issues can be addressed creatively.

❖ COMMUNITY OF PEERS

Similar to the community of colleagues, the people you work with, is your community of *peers*, people who have similar interests or disciplines as yours but don't necessarily work alongside you on a day-to-day basis. They may be situated in similar institutions and have similar roles, but they are not in immediate contact. They are the type of person you may meet at a conference or read work from in journals. When people ask you what you are, you might say, for example, "I am a manager," or "I am a therapist," or " I am a service user," and communities of your peers, respectively, are other managers, therapists, or service users.

These are the people with whom you share many goals and interests. A professional peer group, for example, may be made up of people in the same profession who have the same training and qualifications and to some extent the same concerns about the direction in which the profession is developing. Peers may be connected through commonalities other than professional backgrounds, though a peer group of criminologists, for example, may have shared interests but not necessarily the same qualifications or roles. It is also possible to have more than one community of peers; for example, at a practice or policy level, there may be people who share your interests but do not share these interests with others.

However the community of peers is identified, similar dimensions and dynamics are involved that can shape the development of research ideas. First, there is the potential for synergy within and across disciplines. If one community of peers is formed by people within your discipline, you could develop ideas that are discipline driven, but if your peer community also includes people from other disciplines, the drivers can be wider-ranging. Hearing the perspectives of peers from different disciplines can expand your thinking and stimulate new ideas. Similarly, ideas from other settings or contexts can broaden thinking, as in the example in Box 5.2.

Box 5.2   Different Ideas From Different Contexts

A "thematic network" was funded by the European Union to explore possibilities for the development of integrated services for older people. Members of the network were from 10 different countries, and they all had different experiences of services. Some had professional backgrounds and roles, while some were researchers or managers. Some had experience of all of these, and had moved from post to post over their working lives, and some of them had become service users.

In addition, the members had different experiences of social and political systems. One group of countries, for example, had highly regulated systems, in which care was funded through taxation and available to all. A second group of countries had very minimal provision, with people relying on families and friends to fund or provide care. In these different environments, there were many different research questions.

For the first group, the questions included the following:

- How does a state-run system respond to needs and preferences?
- Is a state-run system appropriate?
- Is a state-run system cost-effective and fair, in other words, the best use of public funds?

For the second group, the questions included the following:

- How do families and friends respond to needs and preferences?
- Is a family-driven system appropriate?
- Is a family-driven system cost-effective and fair, in other words, the best use of personal funds?

These questions are different in the details, but it can be seen that they are the same, in essence; about effectiveness, cost, and impact. Discovering these shared concerns was one of the products of this collaborative working: The community of peers had enabled moving beyond local experiences. In this way, different contexts can be compared and contrasted, similar issues identified, and assumptions reexamined. In the first type of context, there was an assumption that a state system was the only possible way to provide services, while in the second type of setting, it was assumed that state-driven systems were impossible or unacceptable to set up.

Communities of peers, however, can have some less welcome effects. Peers may also be potential competitors and it may be difficult to share ideas without worrying about them being stolen, changed, or misinterpreted by others. A homogenous stance, however, runs the risk of stifling debate, discussion, and distinctiveness.

A community of peers can also be challenging methodologically, whether shared questions can be identified or not. Peers will have knowledge of and access to different types of data and experience of different methods of investigation. From discussions with peers, different ideas for sources of data can be identified and thought through in ways that can be helpful for planning AI studies. The community of peers may also have different goals and criteria, depending on the different communities they, in turn, belong to. These may include personal, professional, experiential, or geographical experiences and ideas that make different goals more pressing and different markers for useful research more prevalent. The community of peers has the strength of breadth and diversity of experience, and, while still having an interest in specific issues, it may take a more abstract or theoretical stance toward the development of knowledge and ideas across settings and contexts. This interest may not be supported by the level of detailed experience a community of colleagues may have, but it is still important to have this sense of context.

❖ COMMUNITY OF CUSTOMERS

The third community identified here is the community of *customers*, that is, the people who fund the research or in other ways support it (colleagues and peers may provide support too, of course, but this is often on an informal basis). In some ways, the community of customers is made up of the most obvious stakeholders in the research, especially if there has been a process of developing a research brief and selecting researchers to meet it. These communities may be government bodies; private, for-profit organizations; or advocacy and support agencies, and they may have gotten their funding through state finances, philanthropy, or commercial gain. These possibilities point to the huge diversity of this type of community, with the common position of commissioners and funders of research of taking a broad view of issues, questions, and policy implications. This position, however, may be taken up in different ways, ranging from a close scrutiny and control of the conduct of the study to a more laissez-faire or "arms-length" approach. Whatever the approach, there will be processes that have been established to regulate the choosing of a research area, the development of bids, the criteria for selecting them, and the mechanisms for monitoring the progress and focus of the study. All of this will be shaped by a background of interest in the area the research will address. Interests may be in different forms depending on the funder, as the example in Box 5.3 shows.

Box 5.3   Different Interests and Different Questions

A research consultancy has developed a reputation for carrying out research in the area of retail, with a particular focus on the views and experiences of the staff who sell products in different environments. Recently, the issue of "staff retention" has been raised in a number of arenas, as it has been suggested from anecdotes that staff are taking jobs for briefer periods of time and are more and more likely to move on to other similar or different jobs, sometimes with little notice for employers. The debates about this potential problem are heated, with concerns being raised about the cost to employers, the motivation of staff, and the impact on customers. Three different funding agencies issue calls for research, and a consultancy firm decides to bid for all three. These are the funders:

- The state, which wants to investigate staff retention and the effect that staff mobility may have on systems of benefits and support for people who may not contribute consistently to social insurance schemes. Funding of research comes from taxes.

- An employers organization, which wants to know how retention can be improved and the costs of replacement minimized. This funder uses money from business partnerships.
- A staff organization, which wants to know about the experiences of staff and why they move from post to post and about factors that might make them stay or go. Funding comes from membership contributions.

These are three funders with different concerns, and the research consultancy needs to develop plans that not only address the topic but also the different questions that are being asked about it.

The example in Box 5.3 points to some of the ways a research plan can be responsive to a community of customers. The general topic may be the same, but the three different customers have different goals or questions, which can be addressed from an AI perspective. The first customer may be interested in a study that looks at the way people manage job changes to maintain financial security and the way the state might develop policies to help them. The second customer may be interested in a study that looks at how staff movement can be made smoother and more efficient by asking about what has worked well. The third customer may be interested in finding out what people enjoy about their work, what makes them stay, and how this can be enhanced to increase staff retention.

Running through these three examples is a concern with policy at a managerial level; in other words, the concern may not be with the immediate details of practice or with the principles of knowledge and theory, but with the frameworks or policies that shape and support the development of practice and theory.

The example in Box 5.4 presents a process of developing a study that was responsive to a number of different communities but also, importantly, was shaped by the concerns and drivers for practice.

**Box 5.4   Teachers and Young Children
Exploring Their World Together**

By Charly Ryan

This project ran from September 2004 to July 2006. The project aimed to develop practice in science teaching with 4-year-old children (Foundation Stage) in primary schools. Four university staff members worked with a Foundation Stage teacher and the science coordinator from 16 schools to

(Continued)

(Continued)

investigate approaches to science teaching in the Foundation Stage and record these in case studies in each of the 2 years of the project. The project claimed that "Liberating and channelling the energy and enthusiasm of young children as they explore their world motivates educators to reflect on and explore the world of their science teaching practices" (Proposal 2004). We advocated an investigative approach to science, in open contexts where the children's ideas could be taken seriously. The philosophy was to take a positive view of potential of the people involved both adults and children. We attempted to make our pedagogy coherent with this dream. Consequently, we used Appreciative Inquiry with its base in everyday reality so people would feel successful and have a sense of commitment to and confidence in their projects (Hammond, 2000). Starting from participants' ideas of good things to do (Eisner, 1985), the aims of the inquiries gradually emerged to suit the range of contexts in which people worked (Clarke, Egan, Fletcher, & Ryan, 2005). The variety of outcomes shows the value of creating spaces for growth for children and adults. Data collection through Nominal Group Technique revealed many positive outcomes and some areas for development. For instance, there was an increased appreciation that observing can be a powerful tool in supporting learning and that learning activities with young children are not "just play." Such findings show that Appreciative Inquiry does not simply reveal the positive aspects but also points to the underlying difficulties (Rogers & Fraser, 2003).

Bibliography

Clarke, H., Egan, B., Fletcher L., & Ryan, C. (2005). Creating case studies of practice through appreciative inquiry. Paper submitted to *Educational Action Research*.

Coghlan, A., Preskill, H., & Catsambas, T. T. (2003). An overview of appreciative inquiry in evaluation. *Using Appreciative Inquiry in Evaluation: New Directions in Evaluation, 100*, 5–22.

Eisner, E. (1985). *The art of educational evaluation: A personal view*. London: Falmer.

Hammond, S. A. (2000). *The thin book of appreciative inquiry* (2nd ed.). Plano, TX: Thin Book Publishing.

Rogers, P. J., & Fraser, D. (2003). Appreciating appreciative inquiry. *Using Appreciative Inquiry in Evaluation: New Directions in Evaluation, 100*, 75–83.

The examples of questions in Box 5.4 show how it is important for AI researchers to be aware of and responsive to different customer concerns (which may also include methodological preferences). The study proposed needs to be relevant to these concerns, rather than just to theoretical concerns, and be focused around them. This is similar to the way an AI researcher might respond to different agendas in the course of a study. One of the differences here is that the relationship with

customers might become more difficult, in that if
providing resources for a study, it may be tempting for
in a way they feel is best. This may compromise rese
dence—if there is a difference of view between the r'
customer, the risk of resources being withdrawn if the cu.
happy can tilt the balance toward customer-driven choices.

❖ RESPONDING TO DIFFERENT
   COMMUNITIES AND THEIR INTERESTS

The discussion above has outlined some of the communities that might
have an interest in an AI research plan or proposal and indicated what
these interests might be. Table 5.1 summarizes these points.

The summary in Table 5.1 gives a sense of the range and diversity
of positions on research, and these present a challenge to those who are
developing research plans and proposals that will be true to the principles of AI. Following the principles of inclusivity expressed in AI
discussions, a plan needs to respect and respond to the positions of
these communities. This means that the process of developing a
research plan should involve asking the following questions:

Table 5.1   Communities of Research: Interests

	Colleagues	*Peers*	*Customers*
Experience and members	Practice and research in specific settings	Practice and research across settings	Service users, advocates, campaigners, service providers, policymakers
Possible goals/desired contributions	Immediate usefulness for practice	Contribution to peer group development	Contribution to service development and policy
Criteria for research outcomes	Practicality and relevance to specific and immediate concerns	Theoretical frameworks and evelopment of ideas	Development of services and facilities and policies to support them

- Which community(ies) is your research part of?
- What contribution(s) could the research make?

The answer to the first question is likely to be multilayered as all potential communities are considered. Table 5.1 highlights the differences in experiences and membership in the first row of the table, and this gives some indication of the complexity of developing inclusive AI research. The answer to the second question is also likely to be multilayered as the interests of different communities are thought through. Table 5.1, in the second row, indicates some possible goals and desired contributions of different communities. These include pragmatic contributions to change in the research setting, theoretical contributions exploring the concepts that peers are concerned with, and contributions to policies.

The third row of Table 5.1 indicates potential criteria for evaluating research outcomes, and it can be seen that these, again, relate to the development of practice, ideas, and policy. The information in the table suggests that research plans may be assessed by looking at the ways they might potentially contribute toward debates in these areas. As Rorty (1999) argued,

> We cannot regard truth as a goal of human inquiry. The purpose of inquiry is to achieve agreement among human beings about what to do, to bring consensus on the end to be achieved and the means to be used to achieve those ends. Inquiry that does not achieve co-ordination of behaviour is not inquiry but simply wordplay. (p. xxv)

This kind of pragmatism will be explored further in the last chapter of this book, and not without criticism, but here, it is useful to think about the ways in which a move from "wordplay" to deciding "what to do" may take different forms in different communities.

❖ IMPLICATIONS FOR DEVELOPING RESEARCH PLANS

Arguing that using AI processes will inform debates is consistent with the underlying principles of AI: It does not seek to be didactic or to produce rules, but rather to open up ideas and thinking so that participants can be empowered to develop themselves beyond the parameters of any specific study. This general statement, however, can seem like a platitude unless it is supported by a more detailed discussion of how might this happen and how might it be evident. A plan, therefore, needs to address these issues, and developing it involves thinking through goals and outcomes and expressing the plan in such a way that these become clear. Box 5.5 gives an illustration of how this might be done.

Box 5.5   Outcomes of the Planned Research

The research will contribute to debates on practice by investigating examples of things that went well and detailing the following:

- The type of event
- The context in which it happened
- The outcomes that were observed
- The factors that helped it to happen
- The way that it might be helped to happen again

These will contribute to the following:

- *Practice,* by identifying how successful activities can be recognized and developed
- *Theory,* by identifying the way successful activities are conceptualized
- *Policy,* by identifying ways successful activities can be supported and promoted

---

Box 5.5 gives an outline of how an argument for the usefulness of an AI study might be made, but a real plan would need supporting information about the contents. For example, the fourth set of data identified in the box, factors that helped something to go well, might be expanded by giving some possible examples, such as the resources available, the skills of the staff, or the way in which reflection was possible. It can then be more easily seen how these can be related to practice, theory, and policy.

Another question is "How could you tell whether the study met its goals?" This is also likely to be a concern of different communities, shaped by their aims and desired outcomes. In other words, a plan needs to be able to articulate the ways in which a study has met its goals by describing how the findings will inform practice, theory, or policy. This means returning to the original questions and aims of the plan and being explicit about the ways in which a study will answer them as it meets its goals. A plan, for example, may state that a study will produce guidelines for practice, theoretical development, or policy and indicate the ways in which the findings of the study will contribute to this by the data it produces.

❖ CONCLUSION

Our strategies for developing proposals and plans must anticipate some of the issues raised in this chapter and respond to and engage with them in a variety of ways, in response to the different communities that may have interests or stakes in the AI study. At one level, this could consist of being very general, for example, suggesting that AI might "inform" the study, rather than be a basis for it. Strategies such as this, "smuggling" AI in through the back door, may seem expedient if communities seem unwelcoming to AI. This approach, however, is a compromise that may not be useful in the long term, because it doesn't develop a wider understanding of AI and it doesn't challenge current assumptions about what "good" research should look like.

A second approach involves spending time explaining and justifying the approach and communicating this to a range of communities and audiences. Explaining AI, however, needs space, and some processes do not allow this, so the general approach, mentioned above, might be the only one that seems possible if AI continues to be unfamiliar to reviewers and funders.

In this chapter, the discussion focused on how we might engage in presenting AI plans and proposals in ways that reach a range of audiences and don't dilute or distort the principles of AI. As Egg, Schratz-Hadwich, Trübswasser, & Walker (2004) said about their research plan, which was presented to a diverse range of communities in different countries,

> One way we sought to manage this situation was to talk as much as possible about the aims of the project and to explain how it could be of interest for all the people involved. The most important criteria for this kind of work are transparency and participation and so it was very important to include all people involved in the process of realizing the project. (p. 20)

Their decision, in the face of diverse interests across countries, was to open up the debate so that these interests could be identified and responded to.

This does not mean that a study tries to be all things to everyone, but it does acknowledge that AI work needs to be aware of and address the goals of a variety of communities. It may also be useful here to revisit Rorty's (1999) argument that a central concern of philosophy and inquiry is, as he described it,

> A matter of increasing sensitivity, increasing responsiveness to the needs of a larger and larger variety of people and things. Just as pragmatists see scientific progress not as the gradual attenuation of a veil of appearances that hides the intrinsic nature of reality from us, but as the increasing ability to respond to the needs of ever more inclusive groups of people. (p. 81)

In this way, AI research planning needs to think through the variety of people that it might speak to and with.

❖ EXERCISE: WRITING AI PLANS

Part 1

Take an idea that you have for a research study and identify the following:

1. The different communities of colleagues, peers, and customers (actual or potential funders) who will have stakes in the research topic.

2. For each community, think through the objectives and goals that its members might have.

3. For each community, think through the criteria that members might use for recognizing a useful study, including the questions it addresses, the methodology it uses, and the outputs it indicates.

If it is helpful, you can set out your ideas in a grid like the one in Table 5.1.

Part 2

Returning to your research idea and using your identification of key points from Part 1, list the ways in which you could respond to the potential needs of different communities. You can express these ideas in a statement: "I could demonstrate an understanding of this by. . . . "

Part 3

Draft a plan that meets the concerns of all these communities' interests. How possible is it to reconcile them?

6

Information Gathering and Generating

Inclusivity, Partnership, and Collaboration

A s the previous chapters have argued, a key feature of Appreciative Inquiry (AI) research is collaborative working. This is something of a challenge to traditional ways of doing research, which have viewed research goals and methods as being the territory of disengaged researchers and conforming to accepted criteria for research. These criteria are largely about maintaining control over a study so that it sticks to a predetermined plan, and this plan is based on an understanding of previous research, the articulation of research questions, and the choosing of accepted methodology to answer these questions. For AI studies, however, the process may be fluid rather than predetermined, and this fluidity may come from the voices of other partners in the study.

To involve various people, AI studies must actively support and encourage them, hearing their voices as they express their views and responding to them in the way that studies are carried out. This process is not simply a matter of "ballot box" research, in which those with the loudest voices decide research strategy. Different partners may have different views about what should be done, as seen in the last chapter, and the art of managing an AI study lies at least in part in developing strategies for exploring various views and honoring them in the way that the study proceeds. This is a change from traditional ideas of research as focusing on "getting" information from research subjects to a participatory ethos of gathering and generating information—to quote Rorty (1999), this change is to "making" rather than "finding" information (p. xvi). This kind of rethinking involves an awareness that much of what is described in research as locating data that are there to be found is a process of creation, of generating ideas and thoughts. This is particularly the theme of this chapter, in which the possibilities for such generation are considered. In this chapter, the ideas of inclusivity, partnership, and collaboration are brought to bear on the issue of generation, resulting in a process of thinking through the principle of collaboration to see how it plays out in practice, largely drawing on the dimensions of "person" touched on in Chapter 4. Along these lines, some issues in collaborative research need to be thought through if AI research is to be effective, and these are discussed in the following sections.

❖ DIFFERENCES IN KNOWLEDGE

One issue that faces a collaborative AI study is that different partners may have different knowledge bases. The most obvious example is a situation in which a group of people, including service users, service providers, and researchers, are working together. Service users have strong knowledge bases developed from their experiences of using services and how these impacted on them. Service providers have a knowledge of the way in which the service is designed and functioning. Researchers have a knowledge of research, including previous studies, methodological frameworks, and tools. The relative statuses of different knowledge bases have often differed, and when the activity is called "research," the researchers may be regarded as having the most important knowledge and therefore the most power or influence on research decisions. This privileging of academic knowledge is something that seems to be shared across nations, as a study of television quiz questions has indicated (Amir, 2005) and others have argued (see, for example, Eisner & Powell, 2002).

One response to this status differential is to try to rebalance power differences by developing the research skills of those who don't have them. This would involve input that aims to give everyone the same understanding of research and therefore make them able to engage in research debates. This process may be intended to empower people, but it raises a number of questions. One of the first is whether such input can really empower people or whether it serves to reinforce the hegemony of academia—that is, whether it supports the idea that academic knowledge is of higher status than practical knowledge and that experience of services or organizations is not as important as a grasp of research models and techniques. Further questions are raised about the way such input can be delivered—the resources available for it and the scope and outcomes of it. If the input simply repeats traditional research models, AI will not make much sense, though if it starts with the models that link most closely to AI, the group may feel that they cannot understand some of the questions that might be raised by AI and place AI in a broader context. Conversely, the maintenance of boundaries between different stakeholders by holding on to their knowledge bases does not seem to support an egalitarian collaboration, and the decision-making process may be uncomfortable for group members who may feel they are unable to contribute meaningfully.

Similar points arise when thinking through the other types of knowledge and experience in a group. For example, if the group includes service users and service providers, these people will have knowledge and understanding that could be shared across the team, and this might need some form of facilitation. Again, however, an important point to consider is whether this would be useful or whether it would serve only to reiterate differences.

One strategy for sharing but not privileging different knowledge and experience is to invite members to summarize their knowledge for others, and this can be done in an appreciative way. Partners can be asked, "What experience or knowledge do you have, and how might it be used in this project?" The responses to this question can be used as a basis for discussion and planning, and a number of options are available to the team. First, they can attempt to equalize knowledge and experience, to make sure that everyone operates from the same base. This, however, as discussed above, may be a difficult and resource-intensive process, and it may actually serve to reinforce ideas of hierarchies of knowledge. Bringing researchers "up to speed" on user and provider knowledge may be equally problematic, especially when this knowledge is not codified and packaged in the same way as research knowledge is. The second option would be to establish and distinguish between different knowledge bases and to carry this through to identifying different tasks or roles that participants might take up, for example, identifying different resources for different strategies of data collection. This option, however, risks fragmenting the team and reinforces divisions, outcomes that do not facilitate the collaboration that AI is intended to support.

The third approach is one that draws from both of the others, recognizing difference and facilitating collaboration by recognizing different starting points, but promoting collaboration in the research process. This option involves valuing partners' various knowledge and experience through discussions in which people begin by telling others about themselves and, using an appreciative approach, identify the ways they feel they can contribute to the study. This may include using knowledge and experience to shape data collection in many ways, by identifying sources of data and ways in which data collection could be organized and timed and by taking part in collecting data themselves. In this approach, the ideas voiced about participation do not result in a rigid allocation of tasks, but rather provide a starting point that people are comfortable with, though they move away it from as the study progresses.

This active participation in data collection can, however, be daunting, as the account in Box 6.1 attests.

Box 6.1   Older People's Research Group: Reflections on Using AI

By Glenda Cook, Audrey Lax, and Elsie Richardson

The older people's research group (OPRG) had been coresearchers in an AI study that had looked at the achievements of a number of user-led services for older people. Following this, they agreed to contribute to this text on AI by giving accounts of issues arising in the use of AI methods and stories when things went well or unexpectedly. Five members of the group met together, and the remainder of the group agreed to comment on and add to this account.

A wide-ranging discussion took place during the meeting, and the following notes attempt to capture the discussion.

Issues and Challenges When Using AI as a Research Approach

Members of the OPRG were apprehensive after they had offered to contribute to the Joseph Rowntree Foundation (JRF) Involvement project as coresearchers. When the AI methodology was discussed, it was met with mixed feelings. The term *Appreciative Inquiry* itself was not something that they had come across, and this added to their "nervousness." Those who had used this approach in other research activities, such as the "Going Home From Hospital, Whole-System Work in Newcastle," were relieved, as AI was a familiar approach they had used successfully in the past.

Key Points

- There was a willingness of group members to participate as researchers.
- They were nervous and apprehensive at getting involved.
- They had had different experiences of using AI.

Some OPRG members were novice researchers, and they felt the AI approach enabled them to draw on their skills (such as counseling skills and interviewing in the work setting) and previous experiences and to build on these when carrying out the interviews. The group felt there were tensions regarding training for the role of researcher. Everyone believed they required some training to conduct the AI interviews. They also felt that in-depth research training would result in the loss of the spontaneity they brought to the research process.

Key Points

- AI interviews provide a vehicle that naturally draws on the interviewers skills.
- A balance has to be drawn between adequate preparation to undertake particular activities and maintaining spontaneity in the interview process.
- Different forms of training, such as on-the-job training, role-modeling, and interview practice scenarios, were viewed as more valuable to older people for participating in AI activities than the more traditional research training.

The example in Box 6.1 indicates that inclusivity in AI research is a process that has to be thought through carefully so that partners' confidence in their contributions can be maintained. Other examples also suggest that it is a process worth engaging with and that partners have found the process to be a positive one. The example in Box 6.2 shows how initial reluctance and suspicion changed as one study took place.

Box 6.2   Using AI to Explore Innovative Ideas

By Marie-Claire Richter

As I began my doctoral studies, I was interested in looking at the organization of health care services and its impact on nurses' work satisfaction and retention. The recent shortage of health care professionals combined with the cost containment and restructuring initiatives had left health care workers feeling dissatisfied and demoralized, which consequently affected the care given to patients. The need to think "outside the box" about ways to retain health care workers and my conviction that the potential for innovative ideas resided with the health care workers themselves led me to the philosophy and methods of AI. As I started to study AI, I met with consultants who used this approach outside of the health care field. They initially expressed doubt about the usefulness of AI in health care: "Nurses and other health care workers are very negative, and they may not want to participate!" In fact, most of the nurses and health care workers approached agreed to participate. Two groups, composed of nurses, nurses' aides, pharmacists, doctors, secretaries, and volunteers, met about twice a month for 10 sessions. The sharing of positive stories during the discovery phase was one of the most memorable times reported by the participants. The novelty of focusing on what worked well in their workplaces deeply moved some participants. Some have even reported transferring this mode of thinking to their personal lives. Finally, using AI as a transformational change process in health care has promoted the emergence of innovative ideas regarding retention strategies and has proven to be innovative in itself!

The example in Box 6.3 tells a similar story, reflecting concerns and reservations not just about carrying out research, but specifically about carrying out AI research.

Box 6.3   The Power of Positive Stories

By Bernie Carter

With little actual experience of appreciative fieldwork, we felt that it would be wise to meet up and discuss our early experiences of undertaking appreciative interviews of best practice in caring for children with complex health needs. Whilst we'd spent considerable time planning and preparing for the interviews (e.g., framing appreciative questions, ways of flexibly responding to stories), we had a degree of uncertainty about whether the approach would, in reality, "work well." Generally, these concerns were unfounded, and our preparation held us in good stead, but common to everyone's experience was the ambivalence we felt about handling the stories that coemerged with the "good stories": stories of where things were not working as well as they could or should be. Initially, people tended to relate "problem" stories, and we discussed the ways in which we had to encourage, reassure, and facilitate people to remember and dwell on stories of positive experiences. As we reflected on our experiences, we became increasingly animated about the "working-well" stories and the effects that focusing on these positive stories had on the storytellers. As our confidence grew, we realized that our guidance was helping people to recall and feel good about times when things had worked well. It helped unearth and unlock what seemed to be a hidden hoard of feelings of success, and people felt that they had gotten evidence of their hard work and efforts resulting in positive outcomes. They often expressed the fact that it had been a long time since they had realized that they were making changes and their input was valuable and valued. Whilst we never ignored the "bad" stories, we found that the appreciative perspective allowed people to place these in context for themselves.

Box 6.4 illustrates similar processes.

Box 6.4   Reflections on Using AI in School Development

By Maha Shuayb

Several elements of the AI were used in my research titled "Towards a Theory of Care: An Explorative Study of Students', Teachers', and Principals' Views in Secondary Schools in Lebanon." The research incorporated elements of AI. Two questionnaires that included positive, open-ended questions were designed to explore students' and teachers' views in 14 schools. Appreciative-focus group workshops with students were also conducted with 120 students. At the end of the research, students were given an evaluation form.

The evaluation form revealed that the majority of students believed that positive questioning helped them to focus on what works in their schools. It also allowed them to feel more connected with what goes on in their schools. Some students felt that this experience encouraged them think of solutions to issues in their school, rather than complaining. They also felt more relaxed in answering these questions because they were not criticizing anyone. Nonetheless, some students pointed out that it is important to highlight the negative experiences in order to understand the complete situation at a school.

(Continued)

(Continued)

The use of AI techniques enabled me to identify the best practices in the schools. Positive questions helped me to gain access to the schools, which was especially important because most of the teachers and school principals in Lebanon were not familiar with the idea of research. Thus, using AI, which looks into what works in the school instead of the negatives, facilitates the research process. AI was also effective in the construction of developmental plans for the schools. However, the school principals refused to take the plan seriously that was designed by the students, as well as the recommendations made by teachers. Hence, while AI as a theory underpinning developmental research facilitated the research procedures and planning development, it failed in bringing about change and progress in the schools.

The positive outcomes from AI research center on how AI changes the way partners think about themselves and what they do and also point to the amorphous nature of AI: The boundaries between AI and everyday life can be blurred, with people reflecting not only on what they are exploring but also on themselves. This "blurring" is welcome as an indication of the integrative capacity of AI and its potential to have an ongoing impact, rather than being restricted to the duration of the study. This impact or effect, however, may be difficult to identify, even with partners who understand the nature of AI, and therefore difficult to describe or reflect on. Much has been said about the importance of transparency in AI work, but if some AI thinking is difficult to identify, it will also be difficult to engage in the type of open discussion that transparency requires.

This points to the need to be clear abut the nature and scope of the activities involved in an AI study. This is not to say that boundaries should be impermeable, but that clear identification of research strategies makes them more visible and open to discussion. The next section outlines some of the methods that might be used in AI and ways in which these can be made visible and reflected on.

❖ ACCESS AND ENTRY TO SETTINGS

The previous chapter discussed ideas about community, in that researchers need to think about their studies in this context: AI research is not an isolated activity, but one that is of interest to a range of different communities. These points are returned to in this chapter, in which the idea of community is shown to relate to the process of negotiating access to a setting. This is not a simple process of getting permission or an invitation to carry out an AI study, as these permissions are, as in any study, complex and changing. Each individual that the research touches will respond in many different ways, and so the process of doing an AI study involves continuous negotiation. People will engage in conversations, offer information, describe their experiences, and work with researchers to develop AI thinking.

One of the roles that may be most apparent in communities is the role of *facilitator*. A person with this role might be the source of information about people and practices, which contributes to the development of an AI plan, or he or she may give advice about ways to approach people and enlist their support. The box below gives some examples of facilitation, drawn from conversations with other researchers:

Box 6.5   Facilitators Contributing to a Study

• A researcher was interested in exploring the feelings that the staff had about their workplace, a setting that was renowned for its beauty and historical associations. A key member of the organization discussed the project with the researcher and revealed that a department within the organization was responsible for maintaining the building and held archives about its history. This was obviously a useful source of information, but the title of the department did not indicate to an outsider what its role was—an insider's knowledge was needed to identify this expertise.

• A researcher was interested in exploring how people developed their roles within an organization. A facilitator explained how this was a subject of current organizational concern, as roles were likely to be reorganized soon, so the study needed to plan timing carefully to avoid approaching people when their anxiety was likely to be high.

• A researcher wanted to look at how users of a health service felt about it. A facilitator saw the draft proposal and was able to advise on which committees needed to be involved, and in what order, to scrutinize the proposal and give the ethical approval that others in the organization would need.

People may support research for a number of reasons. They may, for example, generally support the idea of research and regard it as a useful and challenging approach to practice development. They may feel that involvement in research might raise the organization's, or *evidence based app* (handwritten margin note)

their personal, profile. When research is seen as a mark of progressive thinking or evidence-based approaches, involvement in a research project can add to the status of people connected with it. Prospective partners may also have an interest in the questions being asked and the way they may be useful to practice, and this accords with the principles of AI; it is research that will lead to ideas about practice development, as well as being a practice development strategy in itself. This interest may be focused on particular issues and may also be viewed as a way of raising the profile of an issue and bringing it to people's attention.

These are some of the reasons people might facilitate research, but the strategies they use may have consequences that work against the principles of AI. Some strategies may involve coercing participants in different ways, and this can be a particular issue when the facilitator is in a position to apply sanctions or rewards. Inducing participation by these means may lead to participants feeling that they have little choice about what they do, and any participation will be reluctant and limited.

The other potential response to an AI study can be called "gatekeeping," and Box 6.6 shows some examples of this.

Box 6.6   Gatekeeping

• A management team had invited an AI researcher to carry out a study looking at ways in which staff achievements could be built on. This would involve working with a particular department, and so the department manager was approached. While appearing to be positive about the study, the manager insisted that the department could not be involved unless the study had been approved by a particular committee. The manager could not, however, tell the researcher when it met or who the contact person was.

• During an AI study, a group meeting was planned. At the event, very few people turned up, and those who did attend reported that the staff who weren't there were attending a compulsory training session that had been arranged for that day. This arrangement had been made after the AI meeting had been planned.

• As part of an AI study, staff had volunteered to approach service users to see whether they would be willing to take part. After several weeks, the researcher went to talk to the staff and found that no one had been approached. The staff told the researcher that they had not had the time to do this.

The examples in Box 6.6 indicate some of the ways in which AI participants can express support for an AI study but not make a direct contribution to it. In these circumstances, it is difficult to remain appreciative of what seems unhelpful behavior, but there are many reasons people would do this. These reasons can sometimes be traced back to a suspicion of the study, and this can be based on general ideas about what research entails. Previous experience or knowledge of research may have been negative—people were not kept informed or involved, or the process had negative consequences for those involved, for example, pointing to deficits or problems. The repercussions of involvement may have been serious if the reputation of those involved had been compromised.

For many practitioners, research is not an integral part of everyday life, and their view may have shaped by a number of experiences that created an impression of research as a definitive and fact-finding process. When people are being invited to take part in an AI study, the process may seem vague and inconclusive, like poor-quality research. Because participation almost always involves energy and effort, people may not feel that this would be well spent on an AI study.

Whatever the reasons behind reluctance, gatekeepers may use a range of strategies to stop research happening. Some of these strategies are outlined in Box 6.6, namely, referring researchers to bureaucratic processes that are lengthy and complex, planning competing demands on people's time, and passive noncooperation, where simply nothing happens. These strategies may also involve straightforward refusal to collaborate but may also be less overt, such as the raising of proxy objections attributed to other people: "It's fine with me, but X wouldn't like it." This strategy avoids open discussion of possible difficulties and the process of making decisions.

Adopting an AI approach may enable some potential difficulties to be resolved, if transparent and inclusive methods are proposed. As such, AI may encounter less difficulties than other methodologies. The cautious stance taken by some potential participants, however, may still be maintained, and in these circumstances, talking through the processes of AI may not have an impact, and involvement of reluctant people may not be possible, at least at the beginning of a study.

This suggests that researchers need to anticipate reluctance and not assume that everyone will be delighted to be part of an AI study. Identifying key people and finding out the history of research involvement is an important step that can suggest ways of exploring support for AI research.

❖ ETHICAL CONSIDERATIONS

Discussions about data collection have indicated another dimension of AI research, the *ethical dimension*. While ethical issues in general are complex, they can be thought of as concerning two main dimensions: consent and confidentiality. The notion of *consent* largely refers to the steps taken to ensure that people are informed about the study when they agree to take part in it and that this consent is continuously negotiated. The concept of *confidentiality* refers to the idea that details about partners remain private and that details that can identify individuals are not disclosed to anyone outside the study.

As AI sets out to carry out research in a way that is transparent and inclusive, it may be thought that this automatically resolves issues of consent and confidentiality, but this may not be the case. While transparency may satisfy criteria for informing partners, it does not ensure informed consent, that is, that partners have explicitly agreed to take part. This explicit agreement stands as a record of the information that has been made available, that it has been understood, and on what basis consent has been given. Consent, however, is not open-ended and can be withheld at any point. AI studies may have a course that has not been possible to predict at the onset, because partners will make decisions as they go along. This makes it impossible for anyone to give open-ended informed consent, because they won't know what will be involved.

Confidentiality poses other questions for partners. While individual interviews may be kept private, much of AI work is public or shared among the group. This makes it difficult to separate data out in order to keep the information confidential. Furthermore, in AI work, the setting may be clearly identifiable to people outside the study, especially if a lot of contextual data have been used to describe the study. Again, this makes confidentiality difficult—if a setting and the people in it are identifiable, confidentiality is impossible. If these elements are not identifiable, it is arguable that the study is not an AI study.

Cutting across the issues of consent and confidentiality is the idea of *ownership*: What belongs to the group, and what belongs to the individuals? This question affects the consent that can be given to report on data and the degree to which the information can be kept confidential. There is a possibility that partners will feel a sense of ownership for the study and that this will extend to what is done with the outcomes and outputs of the study. The feeling of ownership is encouraged in an AI approach, but it can lead to questions that do not surface as explicitly as in other forms of research.

That ownership is encouraged in AI also suggests a strategy for resolving and debating ethical issues. While in other models, consent is something that is "given" to researchers and maintaining confidentiality is their responsibility, in AI research, these responsibilities are shared. In the collaborative and transparent ethos of AI, then, discussions about consent and confidentiality can be open and lead to shared decisions. This may involve the development of consent forms and processes and identifying ethical processes that everyone can sign up for. While this does not necessarily resolve ethical issues easily and cleanly, these debates can set out some ground rules.

❖ WAYS OF GENERATING AND GATHERING INFORMATION IN AI RESEARCH

AI research, because of its responsiveness to contexts and events, has a consequent lack of rigid definition or formulaic design. This flexibility mirrors that which is found in ethnographic studies, in which data collection is often referred to as *fieldwork.* Van Maanen (1995) described fieldwork as a "sprawling, highly personal, and therefore quite diverse activity" (p. 7), and Holloway (1997) pointed to its unsuitability for the adoption of a single approach. With these points in mind, the following discussion should be read with the understanding that doing AI research may well involve a flexible and responsive approach to data collection, rather than one that seeks to adopt and maintain a particular methodological blueprint. There are different levels of organizing the generation and collection of information using AI principles, including using AI frameworks to shape research questions and foci and using AI principles to shape research methods. Box 6.7 gives an example of the former in action.

Box 6.7   Collecting Data

By Mary Emery

In our effort to probe past participants' experience with the program, we designed questions using the "4 Ds" (Discovery, Dreaming, Designing, and Delivery). Using open-ended questions, we inquired about the overall experience of participants. We asked them to tell us about a particular experience or aspect of the course that had worked really well for them and

(Continued)

(Continued)

followed up to learn more about that experience and the conditions or setting that made it so successful for them. We followed with an open-ended question about how it might have worked better and what they would like to see in a future course. We cycled through the "4 Ds" a second time by asking participants to tell us about a time they had felt really good about using their leadership skills in the community and followed by probing to learn more about the circumstances of that success. A subsequent open-ended question asked them to consider a time when their use of leadership skills had had a positive impact on the community and how that had worked. We also asked them to speculate as to what the situation would have looked like if their leadership experience had been even better.

We conducted about half the interviews at people's homes or places of business. For those we were unable to schedule for an onsite visit, we scheduled phone interviews. In all, we collected data from 12 respondents. Using AI encouraged the participants to tell us stories about their experiences, resulting in narratives rich in detail and insights.

In the example in Box 6.7, the study used an AI framework from organizational development (OD) initiatives to structure data collection, using the ideas of discovery and dreaming to generate data. This process supports fidelity to AI principles as well as provides a process for sequencing and focusing data collection. As a broad framework, it does address a number of questions about how research can reflect AI thinking, and a similar approach could be taken with other AI cycles, such as the 4-I cycle. The example in Box 6.7 concentrates on the initial stages of the 4-D cycle, discovery and dreaming, which are strikingly relevant to research, but it is possible that later stages of AI cycles could also be used to shape research.

The following section discusses some of the possibilities of using AI principles to shape research methods. This does not include a broader or more detailed discussion of these methods, except when it is useful to illustrate a particular point. It is assumed that readers have or will be able to become familiar with mainstream texts and discussions of these methods. Readers may see some differences between the headings in this section and those in traditional texts. The headings here, "Having AI Conversations," "Written Accounts," "Activities," "Contextual Information," and "Creative Approaches," could be matched up with the more orthodox headings, "Interviews," "Questionnaires," "Observation," "Secondary Data," and "Miscellaneous Approaches" (indeed, many of the examples presented here use this terminology). Different headings have been chosen in this chapter, however, to emphasize the distinctiveness of the AI approach to research, which takes a collaborative and engaged position on data collection rather than the more separate and distant position traditionally taken.

Having AI Conversations

Perhaps the most obvious data collection tool is the *AI conversation*, the face-to-face discussion of an issue or phenomenon. In both research methodology texts and in accounts of AI-OD activities, these conversations can be referred to as *interviews*, a term that suggests the exchange of ideas. In standard methodology texts, however, reciprocity may be downplayed in favor of a more interrogative model, which emphasizes techniques for eliciting the maximum amount of relevant information, the adequacy and relevance of which are determined by the interviewer. Because it emphasizes ideas of differences in power and control, this standard approach does not sit well with ideas of collaborative research.

Carrying out AI conversations as part of a research study has more similarities to AI-OD work, which focuses on exploring what works well in a cooperative and open way and on discussions of conversational engagement, which Zeldin (1998) presented. The basic structure of AI questions remains the same in OD and in research, and also important is the notion of flexible discussion that does not rigidly adhere to pre-planned structures, but is able to respond to participant's concerns. There are, however, some points that need to be highlighted when researchers in an AI study are planning to collect data through conversations. These have to do with people who will be carrying out the interviews or conversations and the experience and skills they may possess. As Bobasi, Jackson, and Wilkes (2005) argued, "Interviewing or observing another is not a neutral act. Together the interviewer/observer and interviewee/observed create the reality of a situation" (p. 497). For further discussion of this point, see Denzin and Lincoln (1998).

The example given in Box 6.1 reports how coresearchers drew on their experience as counselors and interviewers at work to conduct AI research conversations. The principle of drawing on existing skills is an important one, but some issues are also raised here, about the extent and nature of these skills and experiences, which need to be explored to establish whether they are useful to the study. For example, experience in carrying out interrogative interviews in the investigation of violations of company procedures may have led to a style of interviewing that is not useful in AI research because of its assumption that the purpose of the conversation is to uncover ideas, rather than explore them. Exploring previous experiences may also reveal differences in skills; for example, some people may not have been involved in any interview work at all. While this is not necessarily a problem, in that people will have developed conversational skills through everyday interactions, this experience may not be easy to recognize or explore. Michael (2005), in her account of using AI interviews, raised issues that she had become aware of through another form of knowledge difference, that of a researcher interviewing people in a range of cultures other than her own:

> Would the appreciative approach I was using give interviewees the impression that I understood nothing about the realities of their work and wanted only to hear the now commonplace rhetoric on the importance of NGOs [nongovernmental organizations] and what a great job they do? (p. 224)

reflect

Whether experience is recognized or not, there is a strong argument for anyone who will be taking part in AI conversations to have the opportunity to reflect on their skills and the way they might be used in an AI study. This process may be carried out in a number of ways, through group discussions or through more structured exercises. Box 6.1 gives the example of some coresearchers suggesting that role plays could be helpful in engaging people in thinking about their interview approaches.

Another technique that can be useful is collaborative development of the AI conversation schedule with partners. The process of discussing the questions and the way they can be worded makes the goals and concerns of an AI study visible and establishes some "ground rules" for data collection about using a consistent approach, maintaining confidentiality, and asking for consent. When these are explored, partners are also able to clarify points about AI processes and develop a shared understanding of the goals of data collection.

When conversations or interviews are carried out by an identified team of interviewers and the preliminary work described is possible, the AI conversation process can be clarified and agreed on. In some studies, however, a wider range of interviewers or discussants take part. In this case, data could be collected by people interviewing each other; that is, participants would take part in group activity that has not been explored beforehand. This is a useful approach for facilitating inclusive research and may be used to collect data widely, quickly, and efficiently. The questions about the particular nature of AI, however, still apply, and any interview exercises need to be prefaced by a clear and careful group discussion, so that there is a shared understanding of the purpose of AI conversations.

A final point about AI conversations is that they are not simply a process of collecting data, with the interviewee providing information that the interviewer passively accepts. As the example in Box 6.8 shows, learning can take place on the part of both participants in the interview.

Box 6.8   Learning Through AI

By Glenda Cook, Elsie Richardson, and Audrey Lax

Older coresearchers, mostly in their 70s, were recruited to work on a study exploring older people's involvement in policy and planning activities, from a population of older people who were highly active in a range of civic activities. The coresearchers were, therefore, researching the world that they were part of and that they were interested in developing. This study involved in-depth investigation in five case study sites across the northeast of England, which were initiatives that were begun by, led by, or involved older people.

By participating in the research study, the coresearchers were provided with opportunities to find out about older people's groups that they had little knowledge of. They found that the AI interview format was informal and encouraged the interviewer and interviewee to talk to each other in much the same way "people discuss a topic over a cup of coffee." Whilst they addressed the agenda that had been set for the interview, they were able to discuss other subjects that were of interest to both parties. For example, in one interview, the subject of influencing transport policy within local communities was raised to illustrate a point about the level of control that older people could exert over decision-making practices. Developing local transport systems was a topic that the interviewee and interviewer were keen on developing more understanding of, to enhance their ability to change services in their own communities. As the AI interview was flexible, this enabled them to discuss the topics that were on the interview schedule as well as those of personal interest.

The discussions that took place within the interviews encouraged those taking part to talk with each other, and this occasionally led them to develop relationships and networks outside of the research process. This was viewed as an invaluable and unforeseen outcome from being involved in the AI process.

Written Accounts

In some studies, face-to-face data collection might not be viable; for example, people who are involved live or work far apart from each other or are unable to meet with researchers. In this situation, AI stud-ies may ask for *written accounts* from participants. This approach has the advantage of including people who might have been excluded if attendance at discussions or workshops were required. It is also a tech-nique that may involve time for reflection and thought, as the immedi-acy of the face-to-face conversation is not present. One problem with the accounts, however, is that it may be difficult to get people to return their responses, particularly since their commitment to the study might be reduced by their distance from it.

Another related issue is that it may be difficult for participants to understand and engage with the study because the sort of face-to-face discussions outlined above are not possible. This means that requests for written accounts need to be accompanied by written explanations and guidelines as a way of filling in this gap. This may be particularly important if the data requested are different from traditional research strategies, for example, more open-ended or unstructured. This fits with the principles of AI, that it is collaborative and should give par-ticipants scope to respond in ways they feel are useful, rather than the ways the researchers have predetermined. It may, however, be very dif-ferent from usual research requests for data and so will need to be sup-ported by an explanation of the ideas behind AI. Providing this sort of explanation in written form, however, is a difficult task and will always be open to misunderstanding.

Writing has also been used creatively to explore ideas and possi-bilities. An example was offered by Elbaz-Luwisch (2002), who used writing workshops to explore teachers' professional growth. The writ-ing was loosely structured, in that it was based on an outline for devel-oping stories and accounts, and the strategy was adopted to address differences in motivation for and comfort with writing. Elbaz-Luwisch cited one participant, who asked "the main question that arose, what makes it possible for one person to write and give expression to her voice and what prevents another person from doing so?" (p. 403). This remains a question for all researchers, AI included, with the potential difference being that any support for AI research participants is seen as an extension of participation, rather than as a problem of researcher influence.

The tension between support as a problem and support as an extension was also captured by Conle's (1999) discussion of writing as "a new way of being in the academic world," which, as Elbaz-Luwisch stated, "honours complexity and engagement with being" (p. 423). Elbaz-Luwisch's arguments echo the debates that were mentioned in the introduction to this chapter, about differences between science and art and the simplification of life that the former strives for and the complexity that creative effort tries to reflect.

Activities

AI studies can also look at the *activities* of people in settings. This can be a useful way of seeing what people do and identifying things that can be appreciated and built on that the actors themselves have not recognized. In the example that began this book in Chapter 1, for instance, there were demonstrations of people acting with extreme sensitivity, awareness, and skill, which they described as "just part of the job." Being able to observe these actions meant that the researchers were able to reflect on them as part of data collection and also use them as the basis for AI interviews.

different from observation

AI observation differs from some other forms of observation, particularly those based on nonparticipation, in which the researcher is careful to maintain distance from the people being observed and avoid interaction with them, in case this affects or alters their usual behavior. This approach may also involve a structured and predetermined organization of data collection, for example, with a checklist or record sheet to enter observations. AI observation is unlikely to be like this, as it is based on ideas of collaboration, inclusion, and partnership—and nonparticipation, or "arms-length," observation does not encourage this. Participant observation, in which researchers interact with people being observed, allows discussion and debate and can encourage reflection on practice. It can be difficult to maintain an observer stance, particularly if partners are observing settings in which they are engaged. In this situation, other roles may overshadow the observer role and raise questions of positionality, or "insideness" and "outsideness," discussed in Chapter 4. Awareness of this dimension places the information generated in relation to these changing positions.

Contextual Information

Sometimes AI studies may make use of *contextual information,* that is, data that have not been collected primarily for the study, but for other purposes. Many groups or organizations collect data for audit or quality ensurance purposes, to monitor work or outcomes as part of everyday routine activity. These data may be available to AI researchers and can be useful in developing understanding of the setting. The data, however, have been collected for a range of reasons and can take a range of forms, and these might not be compatible with AI goals. AI researchers can't interrogate the data to any great depth; the information is usually available only as analyzed rather than raw data, so much of the work that has been done on it is invisible and unalterable. AI researchers cannot usually tailor the data to the goals of their studies, and so if they do use the information, they will have to bear these restrictions in mind, which may mean that the data can be used only to add some detail to descriptions of settings.

Contextual information, however, can be important in the process of describing a place and time (discussed in Chapter 3), so that other people can make sense of what happened there. Describing key factors in AI change processes is a matter of judgment for research participants, developed from an understanding of action and process, and so the need for some contextual information may not be apparent until later in the study. For example, it may become apparent that some practice development is facilitated by staffing levels, and so these figures need to be gathered, so that people can decide how their settings are similar or different, a need that may not be clear until the study is under way.

Creative Methods

The sources discussed above are the ones usually mentioned in textbooks, but this is not an exhaustive list. There are a range of other data sources that might be used in AI. Egg, Schratz-Hadwich, Trübswasser, and Walker (2004) described the example of using photographs that children in the study had taken, which allowed children to choose the images they felt were important to them:

> Often when photographs are used in research, efforts are made to standardise the images by controlling the background and reduce the bias that comes from relying on a photographer to frame the image and choose the moment to press the shutter. Another approach, as we have adopted here, is to put the camera in the hands of those who are the subjects of the research. The idea is that, since in any photo the picture reveals something of the person behind the camera, then the study can exploit this element of subjectivity by making it part of the process of research. (p. 32)

Further discussion of the use of photographs has been offered by Wang and Redwood-Jones (2001), describing the use of "photovoice," an approach whereby people are given opportunities to take photographs in order to communicate their ideas to others. This is supported by processes of group reflection, as a way of planning and evaluating photographs. As Wang and Redwood-Jones explained, however, this raises a number of ethical issues about consent and confidentiality; for example, photographs may include images of people who are not part of the project.

Similarly, when partners produce images or sounds to depict their experiences, this can be a powerful way of exploring ideas and feelings. Data may therefore involve painting, drawing, or playing instruments and can engage partners in a creative exploration. One example of such creative approaches to expressing ideas is offered by a group called "Old Spice," who present ideas about growing older to a range of different audiences (Reed, Stanley, & Clarke, 2004). Their work is iterative, in that they adapt and create songs and sketches with the support of scriptwriters and audiences and use them to illustrate and explore ideas. One sketch, for example, explores the way professionals can treat older people as if they cannot understand discussions, and the response and comments from audiences is used to adapt the jointly written script for future performances. This dramatization of ideas is an effective way of conveying ideas, but it presents a number of challenges in data collection terms, in that the nature of performances is ephemeral and variable and it is difficult to get a sense of the ideas that have been explored. The Old Spice group has addressed this by asking for written feedback from audiences, and this could be extended by using audio and visual recordings of performances and discussions.

Another approach to creative data generation is indicated in the example in Box 6.9.

Box 6.9   Appreciative Meditations

By Tim Luckcock

I have asked myself the "unconditional positive question": *What is life-affirming in my approach to teaching?* And in answering this celebration-focused question, I have written appreciatively in the form of short meditative descriptions of my inner experience so as to articulate nine life-affirming dimensions of the soul of teaching. I hope that readers likewise will take a moment to reflect on each of these phenomenological-style portraits, not so much with critique uppermost in mind, but seeking to appreciate which aspects, if not all, they feel particularly resonate with in themselves.

Meditation 1. I am very aware of being attentive to evaluative issues of right and wrong. I assess the quality of pupil learning by making judgments against criteria. I catch myself in moments of self-criticism, kicking myself

(Continued)

(Continued)

for mistakes made in my lessons. I am engaged in formal processes of self-evaluation designed to perfect my practice. I find myself making harsh personal judgments about the deficiencies of working conditions or the limitations of aggressive parents. I complain about the lack of adequate car-parking facilities, and I can spot litter on the other side of the playground as easily as spelling mistakes that jump off the page. Deep within, I am attuned to diagnosing competencies, behaviors, and environments, with a view to making improvements and correcting faults in my desire to make the world a better place. I sense in all this that I am motivated as much by my own inner critic as by externally imposed standards.

In Box 6.9, the author has used meditation to generate a reflective response to an appreciative question. This account suggests that AI research can generate such individual accounts with appropriate preparation and support. What needs to be done, however, is more work on what this preparation and support might be and how such reflective accounts can be supported.

The example in Box 6.10 also illustrates how AI data collection can be creatively approached.

Box 6.10 Appreciating Trailblazers

By Julie Barnes

The Identification, Referral and Tracking (IRT) Project has been established by the Department for Education and Skills (DfES) to ensure that children at risk of social exclusion are identified, referred to appropriate services, and tracked so that they do not slip through the service net. Fifteen top-tier local authorities were given "trailblazer" status and funding to lead the way in developing the project and to generate learning to assist the 135 local authorities developing IRT from September 2003.

Client Objective

The DfES commissioned an evaluation of this development work from Royal Holloway, University of London, in September 2003. The research methodology included three regional workshops in which stakeholders were invited to participate in an Appreciative Inquiry into what they had learned in developing and implementing IRT. The workshops aimed to bring together the key stakeholders to explore their experiences of developing IRT and to evaluate what had been achieved. Bringing everyone together for a day of activity, reflection, and discussion was an opportunity for stakeholders from different trailblazer authorities to share their experiences in a constructive environment and to contribute positively to the further development of IRT.

What Was Done?

Three regional workshops were held, bringing together a group of key stakeholders from neighboring IRT trailblazers. The aim was to discuss and explore their experiences, focusing particularly on what they had found to have worked well in developing and implementing IRT across their authority. Project managers were asked to identify and invite 10 key stakeholders involved in the development of IRT.

Each day began with a brief outline of the research and a more detailed explanation of the aims and objectives of the workshop and how it would be organized. The day was then divided into six sessions:

1. Individuals from different trailblazers worked in pairs and interviewed each other to explore their experiences of developing IRT, using appreciative questions.
2. Pairs formed groups of four to six individuals to share stories and draw together emerging themes.
3. Groups used pictures to represent their hopes for IRT and identified three things they would put in a "kit-bag" to give to other local authorities, including advice or a key message.
4. In the fourth session, groups presented their work to the other groups.
5. Participants rejoined colleagues on their own authority to reflect on what they had heard, said, and observed through the day.
6. The final session was used to feed back the learning for each trailblazer and to discuss key points.

This discussion in this chapter of data collection in AI points to the fluid nature of some of the processes involved and also the potential for diverse and different sources and forms of data that may be useful in AI. Such diversity evokes the old legend of Buddha and the elephant. This has been told many times, with different variations, and is sometimes attributed to figures other than Buddha. The basic story is that a group of people were invited to examine an elephant, but they were unable to see it and could touch only the part of the elephant closest to them. When asked to say what they had found, the person who had touched the tail reported that an elephant was like a rope, and the person who had touched the ear described the elephant as being like a sail, and the person who had touched the trunk reported that it was like a snake, and, indeed, each person extrapolated from his or her data on to the whole animal. All of them gave faithful accounts of what they had felt, but their data was only partial, so they were not able to combine these accounts to form a full description of the elephant. (There are many accounts of this story; Schratz & Walker, 1995, describe some of them and the disputes that the story can engender.) It must be emphasized, however, that the use of multiple methods is not the same as a mechanistic view of triangulation, in which methods are used to check the veracity of the data the different approaches produce. Multiple methods access multiple co-constructions of events (for example, what people say in conversation and what people do in practice), and exploring multiple stories enriches them without privileging one over the other or claiming that one produces data that are "more right" than another. Similarly, in AI research, which is in itself only one way to learn about a topic, the aim of understanding a situation from as many aspects as possible may lead to the use of multiple methods and approaches.

❖ CONCLUSION

This discussion of data collection in AI ranged through a number of different tools and methods, including having conversations, looking at written accounts, and taking part in activities. AI studies can involve a range of different methods, and this multimethod approach is reminiscent of the folktale described above, found in a number of different cultures and sometimes attributed to Buddha. Similarly, the use of a single method can limit understanding by providing only a partial view of a phenomenon. As AI research seeks to understand phenomena in the world, it makes sense to try to explore the "whole of the elephant," that is, as many dimensions and facets as can be explored—and this means that contrary to prescription and formulae for data collection, AI allows researchers to be creative, flexible, and responsive to the setting in which a study is set.

What this chapter also suggests on close reading is that AI research involves not only data collection but also data generation: AI research is not simply a matter of seizing ideas and information from people, but may involve a more proactive approach. The example from the first chapter, in which participants identified activities that actors were not aware of, illustrates this point: that AI data are not simply lying around to be "found," but may need collaborative effort to surface ideas in a way that reflects AI questions. Similarly, the discussion of creative data in AI research suggests that the process is not something that involves a straightforward procedure for collection, but rather a thoughtful and recorded process of generation. This may be described as a collective effort, as in the case of Old Spice, and an individual process, in the case of meditation, but both share the characteristics of planning, preparation, and careful recording of the generative experience. As the accounts suggest, this method is at an early stage of development, and more work needs to be done to ensure that generated data addresses AI questions and provides transparency for reflection and review.

❖ EXERCISE: MANAGING DATA COLLECTION AND GENERATION

Thinking of a particular setting in which you might do some AI research, ask the following questions:

1. What questions could you ask in a conversation? How could a conversation help to explore this topic—what constraints might apply and what might the advantages be ?

2. What questions could you ask in a written account? What phenomena would it be able explore?

3. What data could you collect through participation? How could this extend understanding of the phenomena?

4. What other data might be available or generated, and in what way could this be used to understand the phenomena?

7

Making Sense

Issues of Question and Story

❖ ❖ ❖

The process of making sense of information can be thought of as a way of sorting it so that it can be easily communicated. Instead of printing pages of transcripts, field notes, or pictures, researchers process this "raw" data so that it can be easily summarized and communicated. Raw data is lengthy and cumbersome. If researchers don't organize the data, the reader (and the researchers) will be unable to make sense of the information—it will be just a list of things people said or a list of things that were observed. It is like being faced with an A–Z map of a city—every street and alley is there, but it won't help you to get around. You need a map of the transport systems, which is a selective picture of the city that focuses on the routes between stations rather than geographical accuracy. Making sense of information, then, is a process of examining and organizing it so that it can be experienced and discussed by others. Savin-Baden (2004) argued that this process should not stop at analysis, that is, the breaking down of information into smaller units, but should move toward interpretation, a process of framing information so that elements of meaning, rather than simply content, come to the fore. This change, described by Savin-Baden as an "epiphany," involves the process of *reflexivity*, the purposeful and critical reviewing of ideas and responses to information and the consideration of alternative meanings. By this process of reflection, Savin-Baden asserted, making sense of information moves beyond mechanistic breaking down of information to the synthesis of meaning.

When information is gathered or generated, then, there is a process of "making sense" of this information, one that is often surrounded by mystique. The process can remain unclear, and it is sometimes difficult to follow the steps that have been undertaken, and when the study comes to draw conclusions, it is difficult to decide whether they are justified or reasonable. When the study is an Appreciative Inquiry (AI) one, this may seem like an added complication, raising the question of whether AI analysis is really different from any other approaches.

This trepidation can be addressed by thinking past the mystique to what "making sense" means, and not as if it were separate from the questions and methods that a study has used. In other words, what is it important to make sense of? In the previous chapters, these approaches and the part they can play in an AI study have been discussed, and Table 7.1 sets out some of these possibilities, namely, the stages of the 4-D and 4-I cycles, outlined in Chapter 2, which can be used to structure AI work.

The information in Table 7.1 can be used to plot out how making sense of the information at hand can fit in with the principles of AI: the links between the stages of AI and the questions that are asked about how these play out in practice. This involves looking at both the *context*

Table 7.1   4-D and 4-I Cycles

	Context ↔	↔ Development
Discover	Boundaries	Events
Dream	Functions	Sequence
Design	Resources	Causality
Delivery	Activities	Outcomes
	Systems	Methodologies: narrative research and action research
Initiate	Methodologies: ethnography and case studies	
Inquire		
Imagine		
Innovate		

[Handwritten margin note: Is AI really different from other approaches?]

in which the research is located and the *developments* that have happened in order to answer these questions. The "Context" and "Development" columns in the table also indicate the methodologies identified in Chapter 3, which can be related closely to these features of AI. In this way, the sorts of questions that an AI study might ask, for example, those of the 4-D and 4-I cycles, can be addressed by looking at the aspects identified in the "Context" and "Development" columns. In other words, these aspects are the focus of sense making if the AI challenge is to be followed through the process of research.

Overarching this process is the worldview inherent in AI, which needs to inform sense making. In Chapter 4, social constructionism was identified as a significant worldview that informed the ways in which AI research could develop a focus of exploration, with people joining together to develop or construct ideas about their world. Critical theory was also identified as a framework that would prompt questioning and challenges to assumptions and established ideas. Furthermore, the dimension of place or context was identified as integral to the exploration of construction, and the methodologies of ethnography and case study methodology were outlined. Similarly, the dimensions of time or chronology were identified, and the methodologies of action research and narrative methodology were described. In Chapter 6, which discussed information gathering and generation, tools for exploration were identified: having conversations, writing stories, participating in activities, looking at contextual data, and exploring creative approaches. With each of these tools, questions could be asked about engagement in social construction, the context in which it occurred and the processes that it involved. Putting these ideas together, two broad areas of exploration and therefore two areas of making sense emerge: the area of context and the area of change. This provides a direction for the discussion of sense making: paying attention to these two areas.

❖ PROCESSES OF SENSE MAKING

The purpose of making sense of information in AI is to organize it in ways that will help researchers understand what people feel they have achieved and how this might be helped to happen again. This means that when researchers explore and synthesize the information collected through AI, they are looking for the ideas, expressed or evident, that will help address these issues. As part of this process, we might also look at factors that people have identified as being unhelpful or examples that they have offered of things not going well, but this would be in the interest of adding depth and detail to appreciation, rather than being a starting point for analysis.

The example in Box 7.1 shows how purposeful sense making can take place.

Box 7.1   Analyzing Data

By Mary Emery

In the case of the study of the impact of leadership development training on community capacity, we analyzed the data using both the AI and Community Capitals Framework methodologies. We used Nvivo to code responses to the open-ended questions in order to create a list of elements we called "the positive core of Tomorrows' Leaders Today." The coding system allowed us to pull out suggestions for future training programs. The data also provided us with a profile of how participants used their skills. In this regard, we saw clear gender and class differences. Women generally saw their participation linked to helping the community, particularly schools, hospitals, and foundations. Many of the professional men talked about using their skills on the job to handle human resource questions and to support their promotion. They also mentioned using the skills at church and with Boy Scouts. Several were also active at the city and county levels in economic development efforts. One business owner spoke particularly about using his new skills to help him handle customers and increase his profit margin. The one working-class male felt left out of the "club of professional men" and considered the venture a waste of his time.

The data from the interviews also allowed us to analyze the impact of the training on community capacity—that is, did the training lead to building community assets? Responses from some women indicated a strong impact on the building of assets: school track, hospital foundation, community foundation, and so forth. Responses from the professional men were mixed, as some used their skills to support their careers, their kids, and their churches. Clearly, these men were civic leaders, but the impact of their leadership development training on the community may have a less sustainable impact than the training of those who work toward economic and civic development goals or that of the women, who help build facilities and endowments.

In the example in Box 7.1, AI and Community Campus Frameworks shaped and informed the process of sense making in ways that have helped the researchers to develop ideas of leadership skills and achievements across a wide range of participants.

❖ MAKING SENSE OF CONTEXT AND CHANGE

The two areas of sense making that were identified above were the areas of context, or the features and characteristics of the space or setting being explored, and the area of change, or time. This section outlines some aspects of these dimensions.

Context

Chapter 3 summarized some of the research methodologies that have a bearing on ideas of place and context, and these were ethnography and case study methodology. Case study methodology alerts researchers to the importance of making decisions about what they are treating as a case. Yin (1984) set out the processes of case study methodology, asserting that in this approach, characteristically, phenomena are explored in relation to the contexts in which they occur; in other words *what happens* should be seen in relation to *where it happens*. There are, however, many ways of defining a case, and these include the case as a setting, the case as a practice, the case as a group of people, and the case as an experience, to name a few possibilities.

This idea of establishing definitions and boundaries seems incongruent with some elements of AI, which is, if anything, flexible in its definitions and approaches. Flexibility, however, is not necessarily incompatible with clarifying definitions and the scope of a study, and, indeed, the process of collectively thinking and talking about the limits of the case can be a useful process. The usefulness of this process lies in the way that it brings to attention ideas about possibilities for focus, the definitions and form of the case. If, for example, it is agreed that the case is a form of practice, further debate can take on issues about the extent and range of this practice—what is included and what is not. Thinking through the boundaries that might be set around a case, then, prompts partners to think about and discuss ideas they have about what it is important to explore.

A similar process is facilitated by using the idea of ethnography to make sense of contexts. As discussed in Chapter 3, ethnographic approaches point toward identifying a number of features of a context. Here, it is useful to revisit and expand these features in order to discover how they might shape sense making.

Functions. What is the context for, and what happens in it? Looking at gathered information to identify the functional dimension of a context can be a complex process, as it may be multilayered, with a set of "official" functions and a set of "unofficial" functions. An example might be a hotel, where the official function may be to provide accommodation, but the unofficial function may involve establishing and maintaining the different personas that guests adopt when staying there. Identifying and exploring all functions is important in understanding what happens in a context.

Resources. What is available in the setting? Resources might include human resources of skills and characteristics or resources such as equipment and materials. Resources may not always be recognized as such; sometimes they can be taken for granted in a way that makes them invisible in the research information, and the nature of their contributions is not always evident.

Activities. People do a number of things in a setting that may be unrelated to the function or resources of that setting. To take the example of the hotel, given above, activities might include presenting food, cleaning, tidying, and entertaining. These can be part of the function of hospitality but are not synonymous with it—one activity, for example, might involve staff members getting together to mimic guests or, another, to organize the staff annual party. These activities might be important, but not in the way they contribute to the function of the setting.

Systems. This feature involves the processes of organization and communication within a setting. An example is the way in which the cleaning staff of a hotel evaluate and monitor their work and decide what hours they will work. This may also involve coordinating with other departments, involving a system of communication.

Identifying these contextual features in gathered research information, then, helps researchers to understand what a particular setting is like and what happens in it, which helps to address questions about the processes of AI—what, for example, was involved in the process of designing the future? This allows researchers to identify important factors in the process of change and allows readers to decide whether their contexts are similar or different.

Development

Given the emphasis in AI on taking practice forward, the issues related to development are an important focus for sense making. Previous chapters identified two main avenues for exploring this area, action research and narrative analysis, both of which point to the importance of looking at time or chronology, what happened when, or what people say happened.

Action Research Analysis

Action research analysis is expressly concerned with the effects of interventions over time. Often starting from the identification of a problem, the action research response is to generate and plan an intervention, carry it out, and then examine the outcomes. Action research analysis is explored in a number of texts (including Reason & Bradbury, 2001), and the process can be refined down to the following elements:

- *Starting point:* Sense making can look at the setting as it is described at the starting point of the study and the issues that can be identified there.
- *Intervention:* An action research study can look at the changes that were suggested or made and how people described them.
- *Change process:* The way an intervention was made and the strategies that were employed to expedite this are examined, as well as strategies that may have blocked or disrupted implementation.
- *Outcomes:* Sense making can incorporate discussion and description of the effects of intervention, in other words, what happened after a change was made.

Throughout action research analysis, it is tempting to assume causal relationships between elements, for example, that Intervention A caused Outcome B. The process of causality, however, is explored more closely through looking at logical connections between events, rather than simply their sequence.

Narrative Analysis

Box 7.2   Analyzing AI Data

By Jeanie Cockell

It's a gift to be able to reflect on one's practice.

—Participant
(Continued)

(Continued)

AI, like any narrative inquiry, is messy because data are collected, analyzed, and represented using story. In my case, it was particularly messy because I was acting as researcher, facilitator, and participant in my doctoral study of "making magic" (a metaphor for the peak experiences that happen when facilitating collaborative processes with groups). My work was an AI that included interviews, a facilitated collaborative conversation (e-mail and face-to-face) with four other facilitators. I did an initial analysis of the peak experience stories that were told in the interviews in order to seed the collaborative conversation in the second stage, evoking more stories. I selected stories, one per interview, that resonated most powerfully for me, and, by making this choice, I hoped they would resonate for the others in our group. They did. Most of the words were those of the person telling the story. I edited their words to shorten the story to a snippet, the essence of the story. Each story was about 250 words long. I left out filler words and tangents to make the stories succinct and readable. I created titles for each of the snippets. As well, I highlighted themes from the interviews and color coded and grouped these into answers to key questions. The collaborative conversation elicited more peak experience stories, themes, analysis, and the conversation deepened. I presented this analysis in thesis form, including stories from beginning to end, calling it a "magical quilt," sewing the stories together with an analysis of themes and notions from the literature. Throughout the writing process, I sent pieces for feedback to the participants. The methodology chapter described the AI process, a peak collaborative experience for all of us, our story of magic.

SOURCE: Cockell, M. J. (2005). *Making magic: Facilitating collaborative processes.* Unpublished doctoral thesis, University of British Columbia, Vancouver, Canada.

The example in Box 7.2 points to some of the key features of AI analysis, picking up on the points made earlier in this chapter and in this book: that making sense of information is done with a purpose and that this purpose, in the case of AI research, is building on positive experiences for future development. Jeanie Cockell's contribution also makes some other points: First, analysis is often a "messy" process that involves researchers moving from position to position, and back again, a process particularly complex in AI because of the engaged stance of researchers. This makes roles and goals more ambiguous, and so the "reason" for analysis is not the simple contribution to a theoretical framework that is often supposed, refining variables and their relationships into a system of prediction and correlation. AI analysis has more to do with understanding the ways in which people think about their lives, which relates to the discussions in Chapters 3 and 4, in which it was pointed out that the approaches used to explore the world through an AI lens involve paying attention to the ways in which we socially construct our lives and the dimensions of place, time, and person that this involves. This also resonates with the observation of Jeanie Cockell that much of AI understanding takes a storied form. This means that we can collect information in a narrative way but also, and importantly, that we can make sense of this understanding by looking at the narratives within it.

Narrative analysis can take many forms. Wiles, Rosenberg, and Kearns (2005) for example, identified five different themes it can have: evaluation, the multilayered nature of talk, the contextual nature of talk, the use and interpretation of talk, and the aural features of talk. These themes reflect the features of AI research and the centrality of social constructionist thinking in lived environments—that the stories people tell about their achievements can be complex and rooted in the dimensions of place, time, and person that make up their experiences. As Wiles et al. argued, such narratives are both "a mode of representation and a mode of reasoning" (p. 90), in which people both describe and explain their experiences. As they stated, "A formal definition of narrative suggests that it involves events and their consequences, or the relation between an 'event' and other 'events'" (p. 90). This observation points to the importance of exploring chronology and context so that we understand what the events are seen as and how they link to each other.

The framework offered by Labov (1972) gives some indication of the complexity of the stories that people present. Labov identified six elements:

The Abstract: the summary of what the story is about

The Orientation: the position of the story in place, time, and person

The Complicating Action: the turning point (in AI, this might be the achievement)

The Evaluation: how the narrator sees the meaning of the story

The Resolution: the result or outcome

The Optional Coda: revisiting the present

Labov's framework, one of the earliest to be developed, has resonance with AI analysis. If we want to know what people think happened and why they think it happened, this framework can help to analyze accounts in a comprehensive way.

Shared Analysis in AI

One of the characteristics of AI research is its collaborative nature, as seen in earlier chapters. This collaborative nature also includes the process of data analysis, which moves the focus away from models of analysis as being the domain of researchers who have the responsibility of interpreting data. A collaborative approach to analysis raises huge problems, the two main types being *issues of management* and *issues of validity.*

The issues of the management of collaborative data analysis require similar approaches as the management of collaborative data collection, in that it is important to ensure that everyone has a role to play, that everyone's voice is heard, and that the final decisions and choices are as widely supported by the group as possible. This is a complex and difficult process in data collection, but perhaps even more challenging when data analysis is shared. The process can seem unstructured and unsystematic and open to confusion, and participants with strongly held views may lead the process in ways that don't have the support of everyone. Even if there is a consensus, the processes of challenging this and postulating alternative frameworks may not work with the group dynamics.

There are some strategies to consider for participation in collaborative analysis. One strategy is the use of the *Delphi technique* (Reid & Boore, 1987). This is most commonly used for data collection but also involves a process of refining ideas and themes as data are analyzed. The technique was named after the ancient Greek oracle at the temple at Delphi, where representatives of the gods delivered pronouncements about past, present, and future events. This term may seem a strange application for a situation that does not involve supernatural knowledge, but rather a rigorous process of achieving a consensus on interpretations. Using the Delphi approach, a panel of experts are identified and presented with questions. Their answers are collated and presented again, until the answers are refined to the satisfaction of the researchers. The Delphi process is usually carried out using questionnaires, which has some strengths, one being that it allows participants to be involved at a distance, even if they are not able to be present at a discussion. This advantage means that people can be involved when other methods might have excluded them, with the added advantage of being able to reflect on their decisions. If it is the case that following the Delphi process, the notion of "experts" is replaced by the notion of "participants," the technique has potential for AI analysis.

The Delphi technique does not involve people meeting together and discussing analysis. In fact, this may be expressly discouraged in traditional forms of the technique (Reid & Boore, 1987), which moves it away from the collaborative processes of AI toward a process that is less transparent and less engaged. Nominal Group Technique (NGT) is a face-to-face strategy for analysis that facilitates transparency and has been used in AI.

NGT (Delbecq, 1975) has been used in many studies, with a useful outcome in AI. Box 7.3 gives an example of one such study.

Box 7.3   Using NGT

An AI study was carried out to explore ways in which going home from the hospital could be made easier for older people. In this study, data were collected by a large and diverse group, who followed a collaboratively agreed-upon framework of data collection.

When the stage of data analysis was reached, participants had very little time to spend on it, and it was decided the analysis would be carried out in a series of workshops. One of these workshops was spent using NGT to develop ideas about the data.

The group spent some time looking at data, which they and other people had collected. Each individual was asked to write down the key points they had identified.

The next stage was a group discussion, led by a facilitator, in which the key points were read out to the group by each individual in turn. The facilitator asked for clarification of some points, so that everyone understood it, and when points seemed similar to each other, the facilitator asked the group to decide whether they were different from each other or not. This resulted in a list that was then reexamined by the group with the input of the facilitator, to resolve anomalies, discrepancies, repetitions, and omissions.

The final lists were pinned on the walls of the room in which the workshop was held, and participants were asked to develop provocative propositions, in other words, to take the key points and construct challenging statements of practice ideals. Having identified general areas of interest, small groups were formed to take these forward and work out the detail.

The advantage of NGT was that it involved all participants in an open discussion that was inclusive but also discriminatory. The potential disadvantage was that much rested on the skills of the group and the facilitator to ensure that everyone's voice was heard and responded to.

Both the Delphi technique and NGT are strategies that can be used for collaborative data analysis. They also go some way toward addressing questions of validity, that is, whether the judgments made are sound and accurate. While validity is not guaranteed by the use of strategies like those given above, these strategies do make the process of analysis more transparent and open to scrutiny. It then becomes possible to record the ideas and decisions discussed by the group and to indicate the rationale behind these choices. A different team might look at the data differently; however, the claim is not being made that there is only one way to analyze data, but that "this is what was done in this particular case."

Data Across Cases

As well as involving analysis by more than one person or group, AI can involve analysis of data from more than one setting. This involves looking within and across settings to identify learning that is specific to each setting and learning that summarizes dynamics across environments. To think this through, it is useful to look at some of the debates in case study methodology, in which similar questions arise. Egg, Schratz-Hadwich, Trübswasser, and Walker (2004) tackled this issue when they carried out an AI-based study across four different countries, looking at how children who had experienced violence had developed strategies for responding to it. Some lessons were specific to each setting, with its own historical and cultural background, but some lessons applied across settings:

> We found ourselves with different stories to tell about each of the four sites. There were differences within and between the Villages themselves, in their social, political and cultural contexts and in the ways we had used the photographic method within each Village. We each had different experiences in working with Village staff, in relating to the families and in working with the children. These differences are both intriguing and instructive.
>
> We also found many points of agreement, connection and similarity across the sites. For the children, their family (mothers/ aunts, sisters and brothers) and their friends were of central importance, as were the details of their material environment—the beds where they slept, the kitchens where their mothers cooked for them and the shrines/altars where they prayed. The children photographed and talked about their natural environment—trees, plants, flowers, fungi, the sky, birds and animals. For some there were special places where they went, where adults did not often go, a place in the forest, or a pond.

We were looking for something and found something else. Watching the children and how they dedicated themselves to the work, how concentrated, responsible, serious and at the same time full with fun and pleasure they were as they took their photos. All of them were ready to help us in answering that difficult question we brought to them: What are for you the places where there is no violence? (Egg et al., 2004, p. 110)

Egg et al. pointed to the way they had paid attention to similarity and difference, not aiming for easy global conclusions, which would oversimplify the dynamics of particular settings, but also not being restricted to seeing each setting as completely separate and different from the others. A similar choice arises in studies that do not involve separate settings, but simply different people, who may all have different experiences, roles, and ideas. Again, it is a challenge to analyze data in ways that are inclusive of all of these dimensions of similarity and difference.

This multiple layering of the specific and the general makes AI analysis a challenging and a complex process. If our main question is "What works?" then we need to ensure that the answer we develop looks at what works across and within contexts.

Audit Trails in AI Analysis

The questions involved in AI studies have been discussed in previous chapters, including those concerning the development of research plans and processes of data collection—and to summarize, they have to do with exploring what works well and what helps it to happen. Both types of questions will be asked in the process of data collection, but analysis is not simply a matter of sorting data according to the question. Data are rarely as neat and tidy as this, and different sets of data may encompass a range of phenomena, for example, across and within settings. Identifying the data that may help to address AI questions, then, can be a complex process, one that may be made more complex by certain approaches, such as those that bring people together as participants in the process of data analysis. This may lead to a range of different interpretations of data that are multilayered and multifaceted.

This points to a need for a form of *audit trail* in AI analysis, an account of the process of analysis, the ideas identified and the rationale for them, which readers are able to read and critically reflect on. Reflection may involve challenging the interpretations made and proposing alternatives, and so AI researchers need to be transparent in the way they present their interpretations and the alternatives they did not choose. Such transparency may involve accounts of the process and stages of analysis, how it was done and who was involved and also the context in which it was carried out. As Egg et al. (2004) described in their study of children who had encountered violence, AI research is fundamentally interpretative in nature, and,

> unlike statistical surveys, interpretive research is not generally precise about its limitations and places some responsibility on the reader to make judgements about the reliability, validity and generalisability of the study. Reading the case studies it is natural to ask for information about the Villages, their location and history, the children and their families and also perhaps about the researchers and their backgrounds. Only with this information can the reader begin to tease out the ways in which the study relates to their own experience, knowledge and beliefs and so begin a critical dialogue with the text.
>
> It follows that each reader will read the text in the light of the knowledge that they bring to it. The Report will be successful if it stimulates dialogue and discussion among those who read it. (pp. 18–19)

In the commentary by Egg et al., research is seen as a communication in which both the researchers and the readers are engaged in a dialogue. Readers are seen not as passive recipients of results, but as active shapers of ideas, building on their experience and understanding to use studies as a source for action. This view of readers also embraces the idea that they may have different interpretations of data and that it is not the aim of the research to direct or insist on particular interpretations, but simply to provide the explanations for them.

❖ DEVELOPING THEORIES AND CONCEPTS

An important step in the process of analysis is the development of theories and concepts that will link with debates that are wider-ranging than the individual study. These theoretical developments may address the way the analysis can accomplish the following:

- Challenge current ideas by suggesting alternatives or by indicating areas in which the foundations of current ideas might be different

- Support and supplement current ideas by presenting an analysis that resonates with and adds detail to theoretical formulations

Some writers have discussed theories in terms of their scope and range: micro-, midrange, and macrotheory. Put simply, and at some risk of oversimplification, these categories reflect the parameters of the ideas that they refer to: Macrotheories are about big issues, for example, communication; microtheories are about immediate and small-scale phenomena, such as the language used in particular interactions; and midrange theories fall somewhere in between. In AI, there may be many layers of theory development: The findings of an AI study can inform macrotheory about the broad theoretical issues that are background to the AI work, and they can also inform the microtheory issues of practice. The study is relevant not only to the immediate questions of practice development but also to more general frameworks.

AI analysis can contribute to debates about levels of theories and concepts by the two processes of challenge and support. What needs to be checked carefully, however, is that the processes of sense making are robust and transparent, so that any contributions to theory can be made from a sound and clear basis.

The issue of AI and its contributions to theory will be discussed in depth in the final chapter of this book, but here, the point is made that the process of theory development rests on the critical transparency of the study throughout, from the planning and data collection to the analysis. This can be an uncomfortable process, opening the researcher to criticism, and while this may be an expected process in earlier stages of the study, when it comes to data analysis, it can seem a very risky business. The process of data analysis is not often discussed, partly because in quantitative analysis, it is assumed that concepts of analysis are shared and agreed upon and because in qualitative analysis, much has been made of the power of the analyst's "immersion" in the data, which cannot be shared by anyone else. In AI, however, there is a thread running through studies that has to do with moving away from the idea of taken-for-granted analytic processes and making them transparent, in order to share them with the wider communities to which they aim to contribute. Moving toward this transparency, however, can be a difficult process and, as the next chapters suggest, may be unwelcome to a range of people for a range of reasons.

❖ CONCLUSION

This chapter has explored possibilities of data analysis in AI: the ways in which we might make sense of the data. Much of the discussion reiterated the idea that transparency is fundamental, that is, that the processes of analysis need to be explicit in accounts of the study, so that audiences can decide for themselves whether the conclusions drawn are justified. This seems a rather vague point to finish a study with—a sort of inconclusive conclusion that can be difficult to describe and communicate to others (and fellow participants). The next chapter will explore some of the ways in which this might be done and the processes of thinking and planning that may be needed in the process of dissemination.

❖ EXERCISE: CONVERSATION WITH A RESIDENT

This exercise presents some data from an AI study that looked at the experiences of older people moving into care homes (assisted living). It involved interviews with residents, staff, and care managers and some observations of care home life.

Conversation With a Resident

Researcher: So, how are you getting on here, how are things going?

Resident: Oh it's lovely—they're all very kind and friendly, they couldn't have been nicer. I'm very lucky to be here—my daughter chose really well.

Researcher: So, did you choose the place?

Resident: No, I was in hospital, so my daughter had to do it. She went 'round quite a few, and she came back to me and said "I've found the perfect place for you—it's lovely." I knew I could rely on her to make the decision—we've always been very close.

Researcher: So, is it helpful to have someone to help you to choose a home?

Resident: Well for me, I couldn't have done it without her. I would have had to rely on someone like a nurse or a social worker to find somewhere, and they might not have known anything about me, or what I'd like.

Researcher: So, what did your daughter know?

Resident: Well, she knew my tastes, the decoration and things. And she knew what sort of person I'd get on with.

Participation in the Care Home World

Small room, decorated in pastel colors. Small chest of drawers was resident's own, as were two pictures (family photographs). Windowsill had bouquet of flowers and a "Welcome to your new home" card on it. Card from neighbor. During interview, staff came round with tea and biscuits. Knocked on door before entering and offered researcher a cup of tea. Did not ask resident whether she wanted her guest to be offered this.

Conversation With the Care Home Manager

Researcher: What sort of things do you do to help people settle in to their new home?

Care home manager: We try to help them settle in, and they can bring bits of furniture and pictures. They tend to bring things with sentimental value, and photographs are very important—usually of family. They'll tell you who they are—"This is my daughter and her kids"—and they'll tell you where they live and what they do.

Researcher: So, do residents find that useful?

Care home manager: I think they do—for some people its essential. Some people say, at first, that they don't want to do it, but we try to keep some of their stuff in storage, and if they come 'round to the idea later, they can get it out.

Conversation With the Social Worker

Researcher: So, how do people choose a home?

Social worker: The families usually do the choosing of the home— they [residents] can't be bothered or are too ill to do it themselves. Also there's a problem in getting them to the homes—they need cars that can take wheelchairs sometimes, and it's a fuss. Sometimes the families don't make the right choice—they'll go for a fancy home rather than the one their parent would fit in with best, but I think that's because they feel guilty about putting them in a home, so at least they can say it's a fancy one.

Researcher: So, do you play a role in helping them choose homes?

Social worker: Well, we're restricted because we can't recommend specific homes—otherwise we could be accused of having a commercial interest, but we can talk families 'round the basics, you know, what sort of person it is and what sort of home would suit them.

Questions

1. Looking at these data, what stories can you identify?

2. Are the data consistent, or do some contradict or expand on the stories of others?

3. What would you look for in other data to confirm or disconfirm your initial ideas?

4. What seems to help people and their families to choose a care home?

8

Communicating and Disseminating Research

Voice, Audience, and Message

A ppreciative Inquiry (AI) studies may be difficult to draw to a close, as AI has an open-ended nature that can make it difficult to decide when, or if, the work is ready to share. Nonetheless, a time will come when partners feel that it would be useful to tell people about what has been done. This chapter discusses issues of disseminating and communicating AI study findings and how the principles of AI can inform this process. These principles can provide an incentive for dissemination, particularly the ideas of community, inclusivity, and involvement and the ideas of building on achievements. The principle of collaboration means that dissemination is necessary to take AI messages beyond those immediately taking part in the study and extend understanding across a range of audiences. The principle of building on achievement makes these messages positive ones, which, moreover, point to achievements across settings. Inclusivity and strengths-based appreciation make the focus of messages more constructive than messages about risks and failures and invite engagement in AI discussions in a range of readers' contexts and situations. This chapter points to the range of possible conversations that can be generated by AI studies and the different concerns and criteria that apply to them.

The chapter has three main sections, first, a section on voice, which outlines the debates on ownership of a collaborative AI study and addresses questions about whose voice is being heard. The second section looks at the possible audiences that communication might involve and the different interests and concerns they might have. The third section looks at the sort of message that might be disseminated, a discussion about how AI might make contributions to debates in different communities. This discussion returns to some of the debates about communities of interest, which have been examined throughout the book, particularly in Chapter 5. The final section of this chapter gives an overview of different possibilities of dissemination media.

❖ VOICE

The previous chapters, particularly those on data collection and analysis, have described the collaborative nature of AI, in which the research involves a wide range of partners. Strategies for responding to the diversity in these processes of research have been outlined in previous chapters, but this is not to suggest that the issues of collaboration have been neatly resolved—when it comes to dissemination, collaborative working raises another set of issues. These issues have to do with *voice*, that is, whose voice is heard in the dissemination process.

 Shotter (2006) argued that one important difference between voices is the idea of "withness" or "aboutness," in other words, that voices can talk *about* the world or *with* the world they have explored. The collaborative nature of AI means that "withness" should be a feature of the AI work throughout. As previous discussions have suggested, inclusive AI projects have to develop strategies for making decisions on planning, doing, and analyzing research. These strategies are needed to make sure that everyone's view is heard and respected throughout the research process. In the dissemination stage, the importance of the partner's voice retains primacy if the study is to fulfill the principles of inclusivity that AI is built on—it would not make sense to have collective decision making throughout a study, only for this to be abandoned and dissemination carried out by a small and select section of the team. This inclusion can also be justified on pragmatic grounds, in the way that it may help to ensure that the study has maximum impact with as many audiences and in as many ways as possible, and it goes beyond simply operational concerns. Partners can contribute in many ways, for example, identifying contact details of readers who might be interested in the study, but the contribution being considered here is concerned with the details of dissemination, rather than shaping the dissemination itself.

Box 8.1 gives an example of the way participants can have a voice in the communication process.

Box 8.1   Identifying Key Messages

By Julie Barnes

The participants at the outcome workshops said that they were both useful and enjoyable. The days provided an unusual opportunity to reflect on their progress and to hear about the work of colleagues in neighboring authorities. Summaries of the flipcharts and key messages informed the interim research report, which also included photographs of drawings produced in the workshops.

Trailblazer managers and stakeholders identified a number of key messages they wished to convey to the 135 local authorities, to support them in their implementation of information sharing and assessment. These are summarized under five headings:

- Understanding the context
- Creating the vision
- Managing the project
- Engaging people
- Developing partnerships

Other messages included the following:

- Stay child focused.
- Talk to families and young people.
- Not knowing all the answers is okay.
- The journey is as important as the destination.
- Acknowledge, celebrate, and build on what you already do well.

As discussed in previous chapters, a collaborative and inclusive approach to research must address issues of diversity and difference. Partners in an AI study will have come from a range of different backgrounds and experiences and will have a range of expectations and goals. Within this diversity, there is potential for voices to be saying different things and for them to be considered differently. One way this can happen is to award different voices with different statuses. Stereotypically, this could mean that the voices of the more erudite groups—for example, people who have had experience in writing papers—are privileged above the voices of those less familiar with the activity. This kind of privileging can lead to the voice of the service user, potentially the least familiar with academic and organizational writing, being lost in the "noise" from others.

In the situation described, it may be impossible to reach a consensus on the way that diverse voices might be presented, and a useful exercise could be to map out the diversity of positions and experiences of group members. Mapping might identify a range of possible voices, including service users, providers, and researchers, all with different experiences and different ways of expressing ideas. Depending on the degree of cohesion and coordination of groups, the collective voice of the group may be strong and clear, or less coordinated and more ambiguous. What different groups may want, therefore, is support in communicating their collective voices, beginning with an assessment of what these may be. From this, ideas can be generated about how the voice be communicated. An example is the voice of a service provider group that is used to communicate in concise "guidelines for practice" disseminated through networks of other service providers. It would be useful to build on this voice and mode of communication to articulate the ideas of this group, retaining control and ownership of the voice, rather than have it taken over by others. Separate and different voices, however, may need to be communicated separately in order to retain their distinctiveness, while coherence across the project partners may still need to be negotiated and maintained.

Another issue related to diversity is the issue of confidentiality. If the research reported is committed to articulating the voices of partners, this may raise issues for confidentiality: The more detail is given about different voices, the more identifiable they may be. This is particularly the case when contextual details are given in order to help the reader understand a setting—this detail may also make identities more public and confidentiality more difficult to preserve. When people have taken part in a study with the expectation that their identities will remain confidential, any possible breach may betray this trust. In traditional research, which focuses on problems and difficulties, the details of partners and settings may carry more risk of negative responses, especially if the data from the study focus around these problems. AI research, however, focuses on strengths and so is less likely to involve participants in disclosing details that might leave them or their colleagues open to criticism. Reporting achievements, however, is not completely risk free—agencies and organizations may operate in environments in which competition means that discussing strengths can be viewed as "giving away secrets." Thus, in an environment where agencies and individuals want to claim "ownership" of data or restrict access to data, discussing achievements may also be regarded as risky; and since a feature of AI research is that it involves partnerships, the contexts in which partners live and work are integral to the study. As Egg, Schratz-Hadwich, Trübswasser, and Walker (2004) reported, while discussing issues of confidentiality related to the findings from a study of children who had lived through violence,

> The ethical and juridical question of anonymity however diminishes the capacity of the report to provide a commentary that is fully inclusive or socially critical. While it is a common understanding nowadays in research to make female researchers "visible" by using their full names, we did not do so in this study. Aside from the possible risks to the individual, to make the boys and girls "visible" by using their real names was impossible in this project due to the legal limits on using children's names if they grew up under the care of state or any other form of out of home care. The joy of the young researchers in being able to publish their findings within the village setting openly stands in contradiction to legal and ethical requirements of doing research within such an organisational setting. (p. 18)

These points about voice and confidentiality in AI research outline some of the debates that teams need to consider before and during the development of dissemination strategies. Some of these issues, such as ownership of data, may be best supported by a recorded process using memoranda of agreement, formal consent forms, or other tools to ensure that everyone knows what the study will involve. These tools will be developed through discussion throughout a study, but the process of dissemination involves further negotiation—what had been kept within the group is about to be opened up to public scrutiny. This may change the positions people take on dissemination. Formal recording of these positions may take the form of contracts between partners, with their legal frameworks acknowledged and respected. Some frameworks, such as those of copyright law, may need to be taken into account in the process of drawing up agreements, and less formal debates may need to be made explicit. These debates may need to cover the key messages to be disseminated, the audiences at which they may be directed, and the processes of developing them. The issue of agreement will also need to be explored: What will the process be for agreeing on a message, and under what circumstances might this be challenged? Agreeing on the method of challenge may avoid a situation in which different groups present different messages to different audiences, with potential for confusion and conflict. The example in Box 8.2 shows how this could happen.

Box 8.2   Different Views

In a study looking at after-sales services for car buyers, a range of different people were involved in considering what was valued and what could be built on. The group included car sellers, buyers, mechanics, and regulation officers (including police personnel).

At the end of the study, these different voices were heard in different contexts, delivering messages that seemed contradictory. The voices and positions included the following:

- Car sellers who had developed a system for recording after-sales service, which they did not want to share with competitors
- Car buyers who felt that one of the things they valued was the facility to talk immediately to mechanics about any questions or concerns
- Mechanics who appreciated contact with customers and felt this worked best when conversations could be scheduled in advance, to avoid disrupting other work
- Regulation officers who focused on the safety aspects of after-sales service and supported the idea of immediate response to buyers' concerns

These different groups had come together in the AI study to develop plans for after-sales support. They were contacted by and talked to a range of different interested parties:

- Trade magazines in which the car sellers talked about satisfaction rates, but not about the commercially sensitive developments in processes
- Car buyers who talked to consumer discussion groups about the value of immediate responses
- Mechanics who talked to workforce organizations about the potential for disrupted work and ways of avoiding this
- Regulation officers who talked to the general media about the importance of safety checks

Not surprisingly, these messages were diverse and often contradictory, with customers and officers seeming to advocate immediate responses, mechanics seeming reluctant to offer this, and sellers seeming very secretive about what they were doing to resolve these possible differences.

❖ AUDIENCE: WHO IS THE MESSAGE FOR?

When thinking through the processes of AI dissemination, the awareness of the audience or readers and their interests is essential, as Box 8.2 suggests. Chapter 5 showed the diversity of communities that may have stakes in research planning, and these ideas are echoed in the discussion in this chapter about how research may be communicated or reported to different audiences. This discussion explores both local and general audiences—moving beyond the immediate setting of a study to wider relevance across settings.

There is a difference, however, between this chapter and Chapter 5, mainly in the level of detail the discussion involves. To put it simply, there are more audiences here than there were communities in Chapter 5. While the complexity and heterogeneity of communities were identified in Chapter 5, this diversity is brought into sharper focus as dissemination is explored. When examining messages and communication, it is necessary to break down the three communities of colleagues, peers, and customers into more tightly defined groups, as the discussion moves from broad principles to more detailed discussion.

One of the first questions that can be asked is "Who is the message for?" In identifying possible audiences, it may be important to think beyond the immediate communities with clear stakes in a study to audiences that may not have any obvious or immediate interests in the study, or at least none that they are aware of. This may be because audiences are not aware of studies as they are being carried out or are not aware of the potential links with their own actions. The first step toward making such links may be in the way that AI teams identify potential audiences, which is discussed as follows.

Practitioners

Practitioners are the people working in the areas that the study explores. The contexts and settings for their practice may be different from the study setting, and some key issues may also be different. Any communication of findings, then, needs to take into account these possible differences in experience and present ways of relating experiences across a wider range.

Messages for practitioners, therefore, need to be contextualized and include enough descriptive detail of practice in order to help them make judgments about whether they can, or how they can, apply learning to their own work. This indicates a very practical focus to any messages, such that they are not just abstract messages, but guidelines on how to effect similar changes in other settings. The messages do not have to be confined to immediate operational processes, but can also convey conceptual models and principles that underpin practice change. In this way, a report that addressed changes in teaching methods in a particular school, for example, would contain details about the children, neighborhood, numbers of pupils, previous results, and characteristics of the staff, to identify just some of the possible items. From these contextual data, readers working in different schools could look at similarities and differences between their settings and those being reported on and make judgments, using their practitioner knowledge, about directions they might want to move their practice toward. In addition, the report would be able to draw on and discuss theoretical and conceptual models of learning and teaching in ways that go beyond the immediate setting.

One aspect of practitioner learning that may be relatively widespread is the notion of *competition* between practitioners, which can make the achievements of peers seem threatening. The idea of competition is implicit in many debates about standards and quality, and it is evident in proposals for measuring and scoring performance and presenting these in league tables. In this climate, AI studies can present achievements as being common to all, not the preserve of a practitioner elite. In this way, AI can be a constructive way of learning from others.

AI messages for practitioners, then, are important in fostering achievement and developing strengths, but some points need to be borne in mind when developing them. These concern the presentation of messages through a focus on practical applications: ways of doing and ways of thinking, rather than abstract discussions of conceptual frameworks. This is not to say that the practical and the conceptual should be separate, but they do involve different ways of discussing issues, and theoretical debates may feel comparatively distant from the issues facing practitioners.

The way in which the message engages with practitioners needs to be carefully thought through. This may mean using accessible and concise language with links to practitioner terminology and to practitioner agendas, so that practitioners find messages open to reflection and critique. Starting off with an overview of practice questions and interests and then moving on to AI responses will need some explanation of AI methods, but this is secondary to the heart of a practitioner-focused report, which centers on the ways in which the learning from the AI study can be transferred to other practice settings and a range of contexts. This means preparing a clear summary that invites readers' reflections and critical judgments—it is important that audiences are encouraged to challenge messages rather than simply accept and apply them.

Managers

Another group of people who may be identified as a potential audience for AI dissemination are managers of organizations. When management practice is the focus of an AI study, the messages for management practice follow the same parameters as those for other sorts of practitioners. There is, however, another group of managers whose practice is not directly explored, but who have roles in managing those whose work and activity are more central to the AI study: managers of the people researched in the study. For these individuals, the potential messages from AI have to do with how practice can be managed in order to appreciate others' work.

These messages can include a range of managerial strategies that can be shaped by AI findings. Some central management functions, like resource management, monitoring, and setting goals, can be informed by AI. AI shows how people describe the things they feel they did best and what helped them to perform this way. From this, it is possible to develop messages for managers that have clear implications for what they can achieve, which might involve putting in place the things that help people do what they felt was successful, for example, establishing resources to contribute to practice. This might involve equipment or personnel, which may not necessarily be new or extra, but perhaps just reorganized. One example of this can be seen in the AI study "Going Home From Hospital": An instance of effective working was described in which the decision to discharge a patient was made in time to inform the ambulance service, so that the delay was minimized—the person did not have spend time in the hospital waiting for arrangements to be made. By holding the patient review meeting earlier and changing the working hours of the ambulance booker, it was possible to make this speedy discharge happen more often, with no extra cost.

AI can also point to useful ways of monitoring and goal setting. The example given above, in which the staff had identified waiting for discharge plans to be a negative experience for patients and staff, gave a foundation for monitoring performance that considered the time it took to arrange discharge. The details of the AI discussion, however, added more understanding to monitoring performance, in that participants also talked about people who had complex needs or who wanted to spend time thinking through their options before discharge, resulting in the realization that the length of time between a medical decision and arranging a move from the hospital in itself did not necessarily define the quality of the experience—sometimes a fast discharge can be too fast. In this case, AI shaped ideas of monitoring performance as something that could not be done in a simplistic way, and it shaped an understanding of complexity and difference as something that could enrich monitoring and make it more useful.

Similar ideas can shape goal setting. To return to the example of the "Going Home From Hospital" study, this shifted ideas of goals from speeding up discharge to "getting it right": identifying service user preferences and needs as being the most powerful drivers, rather than organizational targets for quick discharge. Other managerial concerns may focus on system engineering, in which processes and procedures are adjusted to support the meeting of goals; on the profile or image of an organization or agency that encourages potential users; on developing standards and procedures within the organization; or on identifying the skills and abilities needed by the organization. AI can inform these concerns by pointing to ways in which strengths and achievements can be recognized and built on.

Policymakers

The findings of an AI study can also prove useful in informing and shaping policy. _Policy_, that is, the regulation in which action is embedded, is sometimes seen as irrelevant to everyday events and distanced from the experiences of organizations and their customers. Policy, however, can be crucial in determining what happens and how it happens. Most of what we do is regulated by policy. An example might be the operation of a shop selling consumer goods: On the surface, this looks like a strictly commercial activity governed by the considerations of supply and demand. Policy, however, can shape every stage of buying and selling, from those governing the importation and buying of aterials, to those governing manufacturing, to those governing tractual aspects of buying. In addition, there are other associ-licies, for example, those concerned with the health and safety of workers, employment legislation, and credit arrangements for buyers and sellers.

AI can identify what policies can help facilitate effectiveness by exploring these in the discussion of findings. An example might be findings that suggest that individuals feel they are successful when they are able to integrate services and bridge organizational gaps. A policy framework that facilitates this way of working would have incentives for working across boundaries and mechanisms for encouraging the development of links between organizations. Again, the appreciative stance may be something of a different approach to policy, or at least people's expectations of it. If policy is viewed as being mainly about disincentives and penalties for contravening policy, looking at how policy can be constructive may mean turning these ideas on their heads. This may also involve framing policy implications in language that is affirmative but still remains part of the policy canon, using language that fits with existing ways of expressing ideas in policy development.

The policy audience, however, can be driven by temporal issues—in other words, the processes of policymaking have deadlines and timelines that mean that policy development has a course that messages have to fit in with. In a policy development process, there may be a period of consultation, followed by a period of drafting the policy response, a period of feedback, and a period of implementation. After this, other policy agendas may become higher priority. If an AI study is to inform policy, then, communicating messages at points when policymakers are developing ideas is likely to have more impact than communicating at the time decisions are being made. Because the progress of an AI study might be difficult to predict and governed by a range of different dynamics, the timing may not always be most beneficial—studies may be going on after decisions have been made. AI teams may therefore need to think about potential policy audiences and their schedules and notify them that the study is in progress and that it will be producing findings that will be useful. Policymakers may find interim or progress reports useful if these are made available to them.

Policymakers are likely to take an interest in AI studies for several reasons. First, there is the *appreciative stance*, which looks at the best of what is happening. This perspective can be useful in policy development because it avoids potential conflict: The message is not that what people have been doing is completely wrong and needs to be reversed, but that it can be built on. Developing policy collaboratively and constructively seems more likely to produce policies that will have an impact and be responded to. A number of arguments for building on what is happening rather than starting anew have to do with acceptability and possible costs. It is sometimes less expensive and easier to work with what is there (although not necessarily more effective).

Second, there is the *inclusivity* of AI, which draws in a range of different voices and views and integrates them all. Diversity and inclusivity give AI conclusions a salience in a range of different communities, in a way that can enhance the reach and understanding of policymakers. By looking at the different experiences of everyone in an AI team, an AI study can articulate a range of views and how they can fit together in a way that provides a sound basis for policy changes.

Third, there is the *pragmatism* of AI, which leads to exploration of what people can do. Many criticisms of policy statements center around the lack of grounding in "real-world" behavior, asserting that policies advocate and support frameworks that do not reflect the real world. AI can help to ground these debates in thinking through what policy might mean for practice.

Researchers

AI presents a number of issues for research, and messages for researchers will need to take these into account. In previous chapters, some of these issues have been indicated, such as those concerning the validity of the research and thus the conclusions that can be "legitimately" (in traditional research terms) be drawn from it. As previously discussed (especially in Chapter 4), "legitimacy" can be seen to stem from adherence to accepted research procedures. In quantitative research, this might mean the degree to which researchers are able to claim that a randomized sampling procedure was followed in a study and/or that data were collected in a planned and structured way. AI research is unlikely to be able to make these claims, as it is selective in its invitations to participate and may involve a responsive research framework, which may appear opportunistic.

AI research may also appear not to fit into the canon of qualitative research, either—for example, not only mixing in some statistics but also moving away from the idea of the individual researcher, immersed in the data throughout the steps of collection and analysis, toward a shared participative approach.

In both quantitative and qualitative research, a premium is put on taking a disinterested stance; that is, the researcher stands apart from concerns about what should happen, to concentrate on what is happening. AI is a different approach to research, with explicitly stated interests in building on strengths and engaging everyone in the process of collaborative inquiry.

In many ways, the objections to AI research stem from a traditional set of criteria that have been challenged in a number of debates. As seen in Chapters 3 and 4, these challenges have come from a number of research methodologies, in particular action research. Patton (2003), for example, pointed to the ways in which there can be a "concern with the oxymoronic nature" of the terms *appreciative* and *inquiry*, such that first term suggests positivity and the second term suggests neutrality. Patton's discussion examined these assumptions closely, coming to the conclusion that (a) traditional research approaches (or approaches to evaluation) are not necessarily neutral themselves and that (b) positivity can enhance the impact and usefulness of AI in the way it promotes collaboration among people involved in the study. While this critique has gained power over recent years, researchers cannot take it as reading that an AI study will be immediately accepted, and they will need to present their studies in ways that anticipate and answer this criticism.

Such research strategy can take energy and effort that can cloud the messages about the findings of AI studies, but without it there is a danger that the findings will be dismissed as the result of partisan and impressionistic inquiry, with little rigor or theoretical integrity. The presentation of an AI study as a "legitimate" piece of research, then, must predict and respond to questions about the validity of the study by linking it to current methodological debates. This can enable the study not only to inform practice but also to inform discussions about methodology and theory. This will involve using the language of theoretical and methodological debates, making the case that AI research has a place in the range of approaches that can be effectively used in research.

Educators

People involved in training and teaching make up another potential audience for AI research publications. For messages to this audience to have optimum impact, however, they must connect with the concerns of educators in a range of ways, shaping the design and delivery of educational programs.

One educational concern that AI research findings can address is the level of education possible and necessary for people who wish to develop AI skills. This concern may be based on the complexity and sophistication of skills and the ways in which educational programs can be designed to address these matters at different levels and to different degrees. AI may be viewed as a component of a broader program that would discuss AI as an option among a range of strategies, or it may be developed as a dedicated program with the full focus on AI. Presenting AI material to educators would involve identifying messages from the study that would inform program design: For example, what does the study have to contribute toward an AI option in terms of a general overview, and what specialized understanding does it point to as being important in an AI-specific program? While it is sometimes difficult to translate practice skills into concepts of program development, such as level and depth, it is possible to apply broad principles of educational development to AI findings. The findings that point to the contribution AI can make to thinking about practice may constitute an introductory framework, while more detailed information about how AI findings were developed, discussed, and applied may form a part of a more detailed program.

This suggestion, that the findings of an AI study might be able to inform the level of AI programs, therefore also involves thinking about content. Messages to educators about topics and issues the AI study has included can suggest ways in which these may be incorporated in a training or educational program. A study that involves, for example, all stages of the 4-D cycle can be used to inform skills development by asking questions, developing action, and evaluating outcomes, as well as informing developments in knowledge in the area on which the AI study focuses. An AI study about the development of the "consumer voice," for example, can say something about the AI steps and skills needed to help this happen, the processes of engagement and application, and also the consumer voice itself and factors that support and enhance it.

AI studies can also shape the ways in which programs might be delivered. As AI is based on an inclusive model of building on achievement to effect change, these principles steer against a didactic approach to learning and development. AI studies engage people in developing an awareness of their own skills and achievements, and the development of programs can follow this by supporting students and trainees in appreciating their own achievements and learning from them. The principle of inclusivity can also shape mechanisms for delivery, emphasizing the need for wide and open access, which may involve developing distance-learning approaches. The principle of inclusivity may also be used to consider possible learners who might be interested in a program, by translating the ideas of people that an AI study has included in the process of exploration into indications of people who might want to engage in a training or education program.

Messages from AI studies can also inform discussions of learning outcomes. While educational programs may have a tradition of being concerned with factual knowledge, the emphasis in AI on reflection on practice suggests other forms of knowledge; in other words, experiential knowledge may be important. Exploring and articulating this knowledge will require thinking through differences in learning outcomes and the ways they can be identified, described, and evaluated.

Service Users

Service users make up another group who might be considered as audiences for AI. In a climate in which service users and service providers can be in conflict, the use of AI findings can be a constructive strategy, building on the strengths and achievements of all stakeholders. This would include the ways the service seeks to meet the needs and wishes of service users and the ways service users develop strategies to ensure that these needs and wishes are met.

AI messages for service users can shape expectations of services in the ways they describe processes of service development and the contexts in which they take place. The contextual details given in a report allow service users to make links between the service they use and the services that have been studied. This would include the possibilities and potential for service development as well as the ways the service can currently be used. The rhetoric of service delivery, for example, the terms *person centered* or *user led*, can be understood by the way they are applied to practice. This opens up possibilities for understanding and becoming an informed customer, and for deciding on ways to approach services.

Customer understanding in this area can also inform ways in which services can be evaluated—not just in terms of different outcomes but also in terms of the processes and procedures that a service demonstrates. This also facilitates informed user choice of services, again, not just because of the outcomes they produce, but because of the processes they adopt. If a service supports user choice, for example, this might not result in strikingly different outcomes—but it could involve processes being carefully put in place to ensure, as much as is possible, that users are informed and their choices are facilitated and acted on. The AI messages for users, then, may address ways of identifying these processes, rather than focusing on outcomes.

Developing these messages may mean that the AI team must carefully think through the view of the service that the user has available to them and the ideas they will bring to engagement. In a culture of data in which outcomes are presented in "league tables," which have a competitive element to them, AI can provide a different way of thinking about services and what users might want from them. While existing scores or measures may reflect providers' ideas of what is wanted or simply use data that are readily available, an AI report can focus on the priorities of users and the questions they want answers to. By reflecting on processes and not just outcomes, AI reports can also make these processes more visible to users and inform choice and decision making in a different way. Rather than just looking at the visible markers of a service or organization, an AI report can also look at the dynamics that go toward these outcomes.

This perspective can offer users a way of thinking about a number of different dimensions, including expectations of services, in other words, the things that people assume an organization will do. An AI report can place these expectations against the setting of others' views of what an organization can or should do. This can also inform ways of using services; if the processes that people have judged to be most effective are made more explicit, this allows readers to understand the way an organization works and the way they can tap into this. Making activities explicit that might not have been apparent to service users can also help in considering ways in which a service can be evaluated. If, for example, some practices are enforced because organizations are eager to make sure that health and safety concerns are addressed, this may make some outcomes more understandable and therefore more effectively evaluated. In this case, the evaluation may not be only about what happens but also about how people have tried to negotiate attendant health and safety rules. Similarly, the process of choosing services can be more informed through an AI study that opens up these debates—a user may choose to use a service by balancing out the different considerations of outcomes and safety.

❖ MESSAGES

Many messages can be developed from an AI study, and the previous sections have pointed to the range of possible audiences that may be interested and the concerns they may have. There are some features of AI findings, however, that need to be in all messages if they are to be useful to an audience.

To understand an AI study, audiences need to know how it happened, so that they can come to decisions about the ways in which the background to the study resonates with their own experience. Thus, the following information will need to be included:

- What is the history of the study? What stimulated the decision to carry out the study, what challenges were identified, and how was the study started or commissioned? This information can be important in thinking about the challenges that the audience can identify.
- What were key features of the setting, such as facilities and resources? Again, this can be important in prompting reflection on the resources available to the audience.
- What were the goals and objectives of the organization, and what processes for achieving them were in place?
- What groups and networks were connected to each other, and how?
- What skills and experiences did participants have?

This information has to do with the context in which the AI work took place and how it shaped the AI activity. The audience can think through the similarities and differences between the AI context and theirs and reflect on ways in which the lesson from the AI study can be transferred to their own experience. If the AI study began with a crisis or emergency, for example, and the audience members are in relatively stable situations, this difference does not necessarily make the message irrelevant to them: They have the opportunity to consider the possibility of a similar crisis affecting them and the ways they might learn from the AI study to plan ahead to prevent or anticipate such a crisis in their own settings. Similarly, an account of the resources available in the AI study setting can be compared by the audience with the resources available them, and they can decide which are essential, which are optional, which can be put in place, and which can be substituted.

Other information that needs to be included about the processes of the AI study might include the following:

- What information or data were collected?
- Who was involved, and how?
- How did people get involved in the study?
- What was the planned sequence of events?
- What changes or adaptations were made to the process?
- How were conclusions drawn?

This information serves two purposes. First, it allows the audience to make judgments about the credibility and validity of the AI message, and, second, it allows them to decide whether or how they might use the approach in their own settings. Judging the credibility and validity of the study may involve, for example, looking at the information about participants and deciding whether the most relevant groups were involved or looking at descriptions of the data used and deciding whether the data were salient to their situations. Evaluating this information may also help audiences to decide whether it would be useful to use the AI approach in their own settings and what changes or adaptations might be necessary.

AI Contexts

The message also needs to be presented with some contextual details, not just the outcomes of the study. This includes a description of the process of the AI study, which is needed to place the findings and discussion in context. AI studies can be complex, as previous chapters have shown, and this makes concise summaries difficult. A process that has involved many different partners, with different roles and experiences, and in which there has been some degree of organic design can be difficult to communicate in a way that is concise and comprehensible. Cutting down on this discussion may produce a short and clear description, but if this happens at the expense of communicating complexity, some important messages may be lost. Readers may dismiss the account as being too simplistic and therefore unrelated to their own experience. On the other hand, attempts to describe complex systems at length run the risk of losing readers who may not need or want so much detail.

Provocative Propositions

The previous sections have pointed to some of the differences in audiences for AI and some of the interests they may have. This means that messages for different audiences may have different emphases. A research audience, for example, might want to hear about methodological debates, while a practitioner audience might want to know more about the lessons for practice that an AI study offers.

It is possible, however, to identify some core components that can be part of all reports, and these include some of the processes of AI and the development of *provocative propositions,* a strategy outlined in Chapter 1. As Chapter 2 described, developing provocative propositions is part of the cycle of AI as an organizational development (OD) tool, in which the processes of AI involve the development of statements that are intended to stimulate action by expressing radical statements of intention. In the 4-D cycle, for example, there are three beginning stages: first, *discovery*, the stage of asking appreciative questions and appreciating what gives life to an organization; second, *dreaming*, the stage in which the group envisions possibilities; and third, *designing*, the stage of deciding the ways in which an organization can develop. In this third stage, designing, provocative propositions can be used to clarify and give shape to the dreams of the group.

Provocative propositions are expressed as idealistic statements that challenge the group to think of ways they can put their ideas into operation. An example of a provocative proposition would be in a project in which the group identified a rapid decision-making process as being something that was valued. Summarizing this as "The organization should reduce the time taken to make decisions" would be an accurate reflection of the discussion. There are, however, more detailed ways of saying this in the form of a provocative proposition, such as "No client should wait more than 1 week to be informed about a decision." This is a much more detailed proposition, which specifies who the change will be apparent to and how it will be evident. From this, it is possible to think through what will need to be done to make the change happen. Including provocative propositions and the way they were actualized gives a focus to an AI report, which increases its resonance with readers.

Provocative propositions, then, express the ideas generated in an AI study in very tangible ways and focus the report on the heart of the AI work: What could be done differently (or stay the same), and what needs to be in place to help this happen? For different audiences with different perspectives, interests, and responsibilities, as previously outlined, provocative propositions can serve as a starting point for thinking through ways in which they could contribute to further development or for formulation of their own provocative propositions.

Local and General Lessons

A provocative proposition is a very local and particular statement that can show how ideas can be developed and applied through AI. Local relevance is important in grounding the study and illustrating its impact on the settings in which the study was based. It results from the way in which the AI study has been developed, but the relevance does not stop there: Lessons learned in one setting can be applied elsewhere.

Thus, the potential for transferring ideas points to ways in which AI can have local and also more general salience. This comes from reflection on AI studies and judging their relevance to other settings, which involves matching and mapping details of settings and processes as well as looking at broad principles and concepts.

A study like the one described in Box 8.2, for example, may develop a range of detailed provocative propositions, for example, concerning what information car buyers should receive about contacting mechanics or how soon a mechanic should respond to a call. More general ideas underpin these propositions, for example, about responsiveness, work planning, and marketing, to name just a few. Concepts involved in selling cars, for example, could be applied to a range of environments in which similar concerns exist—and these are not necessarily confined to situations in which things are sold, but could be relevant to other types of settings, for instance, those in which services are provided. Thus, the example of car sales might inform practice elsewhere, as tension between prompt responses and managing unexpected demands in the workplace exists in many settings.

This points to an important dimension of AI communication and dissemination, that audiences are active participants in using and applying AI, and this places some degree of responsibility on them to critically reflect on the data and make decisions about where and how this information could be applied. According to Egg et al. (2004), in their AI report,

> No authors can require more of a reader than that they read what is written. It is our task to inform, interest and persuade you, but not to tell you what to think! But we ask that you look beyond the evidence we report to consider the questions we have raised about gender and culture. We have explained how we approached the task of making the project inclusive, and some of the issues that we encountered, and we ask that the readers too consider these issues as they approach the task of reading the report. (p. 18)

AI dissemination and communication, therefore, can be seen as a collaborative exercise that involves some responsibility on the part of the audience as well as the disseminators. This takes the ideas of collective exploration that are central to AI beyond the boundaries of data collection and analysis, to reframe the processes of dissemination and communication as collaborative, too. As an approach that advocates participation, this seems entirely appropriate for AI, but it does involve a different mode of engagement that other traditional methods do not necessarily require. Reading academic papers or following guidelines, for example, can be a very passive process, which may involve deciding whether relevant formats have been used but may not entail any more involvement than that.

This suggests that a further dimension of AI dissemination is to accomplish it in ways that invite participation, and this involves being aware of the range of interests and concerns of different audiences and shaping messages to address these positions. Some of this "shaping" may come from the choice of dissemination mode(s) used in the study, which can be decided with the preferences and needs of the audiences in mind. Modes of dissemination include academic papers, guidelines, Web sites, newsletters, conferences, and workshops. Dissemination can also involve different formats, for example, leaflets, posters, newsletters, videos, and audiotapes. The example in Box 8.3 gives an account of one study in which a range of dissemination strategies were used.

Box 8.3   Dissemination Strategies

By Bernie Carter

Our study, which looked at what works well in relation to multi-agency working and children with complex health care needs, resulted in most of the participants becoming very passionate about sharing the results. We wanted our study to influence as many different people as possible so that they could acknowledge and develop their own best practices and implement, as appropriate, what we found worked well into their own settings.

We disseminated our findings through practitioner/parent and academic networks, through formal meetings and informal mechanisms, by lobbying, and through academic papers and conferences. We relied equally on verbal and written dissemination, and one of the main strengths was that the written report was very closely based on the language and concepts that the participants felt comfortable with.

One particularly successful dissemination strategy was the "sharing workshop." We invited all of our participants (parents, children, health care and social care professionals, and people from other agencies) to this workshop and developed the program in collaboration with them. Primarily, the workshop focused on why the guidelines we had produced were so important and why "things working well" made such a difference, not only to the children's/families' lives but also to the lives of people providing services.

Each participant was encouraged to invite two guests whom they wished to influence and hear the findings. The parents' guest list included family members, service commissioners, leads for children's services, school bus drivers, and people providing direct care for their children. The

(Continued)

(Continued)

"professionals" guest list was equally diverse and included politicians, people developing new services, and colleagues from other agencies. These personal invitations were hard to refuse and effectively resulted in an extensive and diverse circulation list, devised by the participants and clearly reaching out and touching those people felt to be key in helping to make "things work better."

By working with the participants throughout the dissemination phase, we believe that we reached many more people than we would have with a traditional approach and that we reached them in a way that was consonant with the spirit of the study.

❖ CONCLUSION

The choice of media and format may be based on the preferences and access of different audiences, which can facilitate engagement with the material in terms of usability. The choice of appropriate dissemination modes may also foster a spirit of thoughtful and responsive collaboration, in which audiences are invited not to just read and use material but also to comment, adapt, and actively participate in future development. This involves a commitment to the AI study beyond the time of dissemination and so must be thought through if it is to be attempted and strategies developed. What is certain is that the use of appropriate dissemination strategies is an approach that supports and enhances the principles of AI study, and it should be encouraged for this reason alone.

❖ EXERCISE 1: DIFFERENT AUDIENCES

1. How would you disseminate your study to the following people:
   - Practitioners
   - Policymakers
   - Researchers

2. What would be the focus and format of each strategy?

❖ EXERCISE 2: DRAWING A DISSEMINATION TREE

Draw a "dissemination tree," with branches for different audiences. The central trunk should contain all possible messages, with each branch designating one message for a particular audience. These may be further subdivided into smaller branches if the messages are more complex. The tree in the figure below gives an idea of how this might look: a central trunk of different messages, with branches. There are three branches here, which might represent messages for (1) practitioners (2) service users, and (3) managers. The leaves can represent the different messages and groups arising from each branch.

9

Research for Change

Ways to Go

I n a final chapter in a book, it is tempting to try to end with definitive statements, conclusions, and clear statements about the way forward. In this book, however, this sort of certainty doesn't feel right, given the host of questions and issues that have been raised throughout these pages. Opting for neat and tidy conclusions seems to be incongruent with many of the debates in Appreciative Inquiry (AI) and the valuable areas that AI has opened up for discussion, about the ways people can learn about themselves and each other, and the processes and outcomes that this can involve. These discussions are still very much active and open, and in this sense, the words of Keats, in a letter to a friend (1817), strike many chords when he described: "Negative Capability, that is, when a man is capable of being in uncertainties, mysteries, doubts, without any irritable reaching after fact and reason" (personal letter, available at http://www.mrbauld.com/negcap.html).

This is not a counsel of passive despair and confusion, but a simple acknowledgment that some areas cannot not be easily tidied up without doing a disservice to the creative and constructive debates that they arise from and engender. AI seems to be one of those areas, and so this final chapter will try to avoid presenting concluding comments about AI as if it were possible to be fixed about the way in which AI should develop and, instead, will open up some of the possibilities that can be identified.

Another temptation to avoid is what Gergen (2003) called "the general tendency over the past several decades to remain fixed within the ritual dance of attack and counter-attack" (p. 40), in which different theories and ideas fight for supremacy, with the assumption that only one can win. The notion that the development of ideas is essentially a battle has some strengths, in the way that it focuses the mind on looking at rationales and justifications. It can also, however, lock us into a polarized world, where choices are limited and integration of different ideas becomes impossible. Rather than conclude by reiterating the arguments for AI and against other models of research and development, these final comments will try to avoid such a combative discussion. Rather than arguing that AI is "better" than any other approach and that other approaches are deficient in some ways, it may be more useful to think through what place AI may have in developing practice and knowledge. In Chapter 6, the story of Buddha and the elephant was described, and how different methods may lead to fragmentary understanding. This metaphor can be extended to different methodologies, the concepts and theories that drive goals and foci of investigation, in that each methodology can shed a different light on a phenomenon and contribute toward putting together a wider picture. AI, then, is not offered as the only methodology that can be used, but as one that is particularly useful for exploring the potential for building on achievement or, as Sheila McNamee (2003) put it, inviting participants into "co-ordinating a generative future together" (p. 24).

❖ THE INTEGRATION OF THEORY AND PRACTICE

Another temptation is to return to the traditional separation of theory and practice, discernable in many texts, which treat them as two separate discussions. While this might make writing easier, as the two arenas each have their different conventions and processes, it does not reflect the integration that is at the heart of this book. This idea of bringing theory and practice together is a fundamental and essential one. It reflects the ideas of change and development that are evident throughout this book, as ways of learning about the "real world" of action, experience, and practice have been proposed through the use of AI as a research framework. This has also involved predicting and explaining possible contrasts and differences between an AI research approach and more traditional methodologies that have been built on the idea of disengagement as a hallmark of "good" research. Disengagement, however, makes research, though it may meet traditional criteria, distant from the pressing issues and experiences that practitioners meet every day.

This book attempts a move toward bringing research, theory, and practice closer together by explicating the links between them. There has been a long tradition of thinking about theory and practice as being different sorts of activity, with research being seen as closer to theory than to practice. On one hand, there was the "swampy lowland" of practice and, on the other, the esoteric "high ground" of academic debate, with a huge conceptual and experiential gulf between them (Schön, 1987). Figure 9.1 illustrates this process, with the people at the bottom of the triangle, the users of services, being the most numerous and the least powerful.

Such ideas have been challenged over time, with Lewin (1945) asserting that "there is nothing so practical as a good theory" (p. 129). The idea that theories and practice are intimately related has also been reflected in many discussions of methodology, in which the criteria used to judge the merit of the study are not abstract ones about research techniques, but are rather about utility, the ways the study can inform or has informed practice. Discussions of action research, for example, have pointed to the ways in which this type of research responds to and addresses practice questions. Action research has been, in many ways, a forerunner in the journey toward practice relevance. Relevance does not lie just in the answering of practice questions, however, but in the way that thinking about practice is

Figure 9.1   Traditional Hierarchy of Theory Development

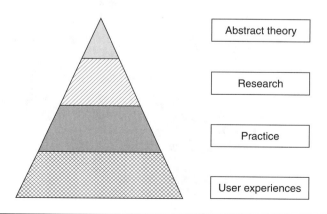

challenged. Critical theory, for example, can prompt audiences to question and challenge many long-held assumptions. In similar ways, AI can contribute to practice by responding to practice issues, focusing on achievements and how they can be built on, and also by challenging ideas about our world, particularly by encouraging people to look at the world through an appreciative lens, rather than one that emphasizes problems and failures. Exploring achievements and developing theoretical ideas about how and why some things work, then, can be very useful in taking practice forward.

This issue of integration has been evident in previous chapters that have described the history of AI and the ways in which it has developed. Figure 9.2 gives an indication of how this could be shown.

These chapters have threads of research and organizational development (OD) running throughout them, historically having distinct and differing principles and questions but also reflecting the way AI stands as an exemplar of the integration of research and practice. Rather than see the

Figure 9.2   Integrated Model of Theory Development

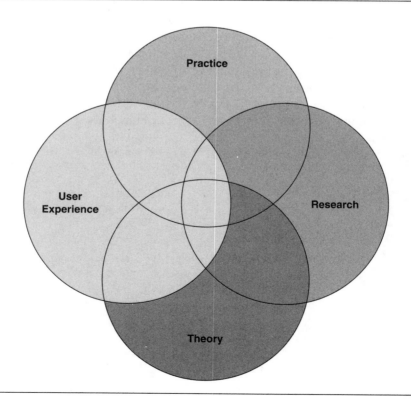

two as disengaged from each other, AI has the potential to bring them together. The following examples indicate how this might happen. Box 9.1 recounts how involving laypeople in inspections was explored through the use of AI. Box 9.2 gives an example of the way AI opened up ideas of leadership to development and discussion.

Box 9.1   Client Objective

By Julie Barnes

The National Care Standards Commission (NCSC) commissioned research into the effectiveness of deploying laypeople on inspection teams. The research involved a range of methods, including postal surveys of service users, service providers, NCSC staff, and lay assessors; interviews and group meetings with stakeholders; and an evaluation workshop with a group of stakeholders using AI.

What Was Done?

A 1-day workshop was held with service providers, lay assessors, and NCSC staff to accomplish the following:

- Explore the unique contributions of lay assessors to the inspection process and to the lives of service users
- Identify examples of past success and areas for improvement
- Discover which aspects of current practice stakeholders would like to see in the future

Short introductory presentations from each stakeholder group were followed by interviews in pairs and work in small groups to discover and share stories about positive experiences of working as, or with, lay assessors. Themes from stories were highlighted on flipcharts and posted on walls. Participants prioritized these for the future, and in later sessions worked together to envision an ideal future and identify three key messages for the NCSC board. These were drawn and summarized in short sentences.

Outcomes

Participants worked together to identify the things they valued most about being, or working with, lay assessors and the positive contributions lay assessors make to inspections. Some of the key points included their roles in the following:

(Continued)

(Continued)

- Bringing independence and transparency to inspections
- Having time to observe care and talk to service users informally
- Being a second pair of eyes and ears
- Working with inspectors to protect vulnerable service users

Issues for development were also raised, and a wealth of material was gathered, shared, and prioritized by the group.

The use of methods developed from AI was considered to be very effective in this evaluation. Participants with very different perspectives on this subject worked enthusiastically together, generated important information that complemented material gathered in other ways, and created a very enjoyable working experience.

Box 9.2   Developing Theory and Methodology

By Mary Emery

The data from our survey encouraged us to ask questions about what is leadership and how is it developed. Today we see leadership as something that can be taught and enhanced through the development of leadership programs. Yet many of these programs lack an explicit theory of change (Pigg, 1999). Current content borrows from both the theory of leadership as a set of behaviors, attitudes, and actions that can be learned, as well as a more constructionist approach, such as that described by Pigg (1999). Ospina and Schall (2001) described how concepts of leadership have continued to morph as they change from "reflecting the values and assumptions of the industrial model . . . goal oriented . . . individualistic . . . utilitarian and materialistic . . . rationalistic, technocratic, linear. . . ." They contrasted this with a postmodern focus on "collaboration, common good, global concern, diversity and pluralism . . ." In applying a constructionist approach, they view leadership as "both a social construct and a process" (p. 1). Pigg (1999) described such an approach as follows:

If community leaders (1) share a common, generalized purpose, (2) are able to work together in ways that leverage existing assets (collaborate), (3) possess a sense of individual and collective efficacy, and (4) possess a broad knowledge of the community and its civic decision-making process(es), then there will result an increased civic capacity for local self governance (community action) leading to satisfying community needs and achieving community success. (p. 196)

Our analysis of the leadership development program in 1987 indicates that leadership development, such as Tomorrow's Leaders Today, that focuses on increasing skills and access to resources does lack a clear theoretical basis. If we see leadership development from the constructionist approach, these programs must include opportunities for individuals to co-construct a vision of leadership and its impact on community explicit to place.

Bibliography

Pigg, K. E. (1999). Community leadership and community theory: A practical synthesis. *Journal of the Community Development Society, 30*(2), 196–212.

Ospina, S., & Schall, E. (2001). *Perspectives on leadership: Our approach to research and documentation for the leadership for a changing world program.* Retrieved March 3, 2006, from http://www.leadershiplearning.org/community/files/download?version_id=1198

Emery, M., & Floram, C. (in press). Spiraling up: Mapping community transformation using the community capital framework. *Journal of the Community Development Society.*

Bringing research and practice together seems like a potentially productive way forward, but there are some important points to consider. Separating research and practice may be useful in the ways this can reflect and enhance distinctiveness, allowing both to develop their own goals, methods, and criteria. "Uncontaminated" by external considerations, criteria may flourish when given the opportunity to develop in a focused way, rather than trying to respond to a wider range of interests and views. Such focused development, however, runs counter to many ideas about research and practice, which view them as being fundamentally connected. In other words, there is the idea that practice should be informed by research, and research informed by practice. As Stevenson (2005) argued, however, "Detached theories . . . lack relevance for everyday practice and so sustain the theory-practice gap. . . . Theories tend to see practice as fixed or fixable, rather than being enacted in a state of flux" (p. 196). This makes an important point about the use of theory as a tool to "fix" broken or inadequate practice, rather than as something that could be part of our concepts of practice. It also makes an important point about practice: It is in a state of flux, responsive and changing in different contexts and constructions.

❖ STRUCTURE OF THIS CHAPTER

To explore these issues in more depth, the various contributions that AI can make to both OD and research are first revisited. This refers back the first chapters of this book, which describe in some detail the use of

AI in OD and its emergent use in research. Only brief summaries will be given here, focusing on central ideas and messages. From this, the chapter goes on to explore some of the debates on "practice theory" that have been discussed in the literature and some of the research frameworks that have been developed, that is, action research and the coordinated management of meaning (CMM) frameworks, and that move the worlds of theory and practice together.

In looking at these frameworks, AI is placed alongside them as a similar development, and some fundamental issues are also outlined. These involve an exploration of the philosophical basis of action research, CMM, and AI, that is, the pragmatist philosophy that underpins these frameworks and gives them direction and places the bringing together of theory and practice at the center. In pragmatist philosophy, theory is not something that is developed separately from action and then applied to it; rather, theory is integral to action—there is no theory without action and no action without theory. Current pragmatist concerns have focused on ideas of "redescription"; by inviting people to think about and describe their world differently, behavior and activity are also shaped. This pragmatist concern with language is viewed in relation to some of the concerns that have led to the development of AI as an OD approach: The process of appreciation involves thinking and talking about the world differently, and this can generate different ideas about the future.

Returning to the title of this book, *Appreciative Inquiry: Research for Change*, the discussion points to two connected forms of change. The first is *change in practice,* and this book has pointed to the manner in which AI can contribute to this process by exploring change and development in ways that are reflective of and integral to practice, paying attention to the real-life world of practice, with its multiple participants and breadth of interest. The second form *is change in research,* the way that it is carried out and evaluated, and this idea has been expressed throughout the book in discussions about audiences and communities. These two forms of change are intimately related: Change in practice depends on change in research, and change in research contributes to change in practice—it's difficult to think of one without the other. With this connection in mind, the following discussions temporarily and reluctantly consider practice and research separately.

❖ AI CONTRIBUTION TO OD

The AI writing about OD emphasizes the ways that AI can contribute to innovation, change, and sustaining achievement. Beginning with the observation that many organizations are driven by avoiding problems and complaints, AI has taken a different stance. By explicitly recognizing that organizations have strengths that can be built on, AI attempts to discover and appreciate what works well. This process of discovery is an open one, embracing all of the practices of an organization and all of the people who work in it. This leads to the generation of ideas about how this process can be facilitated, which can take many forms, including the generation of goals, the identification of skills, and the support needed for innovation.

The process of discovery in OD usually begins with a *commissioning process*, in which people within an organization decide to undertake some AI work. This can happen for a number of reasons; for example, their experiences with other OD approaches concentrated on problem solving. These experiences may have had an impact, but may also have left people with a sense that their organization is beset with problems and difficulties. Thus, the positive emphasis of AI can be seen as complementary, a potential alternative, or at least worth a try.

The commissioning process sets up a particular context for AI work. First, there is some degree of support within the organization. This can be a complicated situation, as those with the power to begin the AI process are not necessarily in accord with those who will be involved in subsequent AI developments (this subject was particularly discussed in Chapter 4, about planning research, and in Chapter 8, about communicating research, in which voice and interest were explored). Such complexities have to be taken into account in carrying out AI projects, whether the team of individuals leading AI are external or internal facilitators.

This observation about starting AI projects also makes reference to other dimensions of AI as an OD approach. The starting point in AI work is real-life activity and practice, focused on specific issues and contexts; its central concerns are the particular issues facing the organization carrying out the AI work. AI work may expand this original interest, but the heart of the work remains in the particular context of the organization. This may also have implications for the scope of the AI work, concentrating on the particular setting and the processes within it, and implications for dissemination, such that the learning from the AI work may not be spread to other organizations, but kept to the organization that generated the AI work. This may happen for competitive reasons; for example, people in an organization may feel reluctant to disclose their development strategies to others, or they may see their situations as being unique and the issues they face as being very specific to them.

❖ AI CONTRIBUTION TO RESEARCH

The OD use of AI can be contrasted with research use in a number of ways, and one of these is the degree to which AI research is characterized by its public nature, compared with the private, organization-specific flavor of OD. Rather than being commissioned by a particular organization, AI research may be stimulated by questions and interests outside or across organizations. These external drivers fit with the notion of broader conceptual or theoretical interests: The interest is not just in how organization X does Y, but, more generally, in the ideas about how Y is done. In other words, this interest may not stem from immediate issues in practitioners' work, but from more general interests in how issues can be thought about.

Thus, AI research enjoys a degree of freedom in that it can explore questions outside the boundaries of specific commissioning organizations and speak to and for a wider range of audiences than those in a particular organization. This brings into play a range of criteria for research quality, as Chapter 5 described. While these criteria may have a number of limitations, they do point to the idea of research as a broad endeavor, with peer and public scrutiny being important in the verification of studies, rather than merely restricted local utility and relevance.

AI research even enjoys some freedom from its own conventions and principles, as the idea of contribution to development loses some of its primacy and the idea of contribution to knowledge is strengthened. An example can be found in Sarah Michaels's (2005) work, in which she explored the use of AI as an interview tool. Michaels related that her research involved a single interview with leaders of a number of different organizations and did not have the usual AI sustained and exclusive contact and goal of change. Her approach was to see the interviews as being similar to the "Discovery" phase of the 4-D cycle of AI. Despite her concern that an AI approach would be unsustainable and seen as irrelevant to interviewees in difficult circumstances, she found that they were eager to tell their stories, exhibiting relatively less defensiveness and offering relatively more "unrehearsed" information.

AI, then, can be viewed as making a contribution to research methodology in the way that it challenges research ideas about bias and subjectivity and points to strategies for maximizing data collection. Perhaps less pragmatically, AI also challenges research ideas about the desirability of distance and disengagement with "the field," showing how engagement can contribute to the development of knowledge and also how traditional structures of power and influence, in which "science" is seen as having more status than practice, can move toward a more open and democratic endeavor, with shared responsibilities and benefits. This can be a move away from traditional research, in which studies are led by specific individuals who take responsibility for them, to an idea of collaborative research, in which direction and responsibilities are shared among participants.

❖ CONNECTING RESEARCH AND DEVELOPMENT

This distinction between AI as an OD strategy and AI as a research approach might be criticized as being artificial and unhelpful. It separates research from practice in ways that make it difficult to make connections between different worlds: the world of practice, with immediate practical concerns, and the esoteric world of theory and research, in which disengaged concerns about academic attainment have priority. As Schön (1983) described it, the world of practice may be seen as a "swampy lowland," while theory is seen as occupying a "high ground," where life is neat and tidy.

This differentiation can in part be traced back to the discussions of truth and knowledge, which took up much time and energy in the debates between Greek philosophers and have cast a shadow over many subsequent debates and discussions. In the time of the philosophers, work was regarded as low status, described by Dewey (Dewey 1929/1960) as "onerous, toilsome, associated with a primeval curse, done under the pressure of necessity, while intellectual activity is associated with leisure" (pp. 4–5). Practice, then, had low status because of its association with the menial but, in addition, was viewed as being changeable and dependant on context and circumstances. This perspective made practice look very different from ideas of "truth" in the eyes of the Greek philosophers. Their concept of "truth," and what could therefore be known with certainty, embodied something eternal and unchanging, in the way that the laws of nature that governed the movement of the stars were thought to be unchanging. "Truth" represented a Platonic ideal that excluded notions of contingent practice, which changed according to circumstances and contexts (Cronen, 2001, p. 15). This idea of certainty gave rise to ideas about how a stable foundation for knowing about the world could be discovered, a quest that led to a concern with "objectivity," that is, the observation of the world without the attachment or engagement that would make this investigation responsive and reactive (and therefore changeable, rather than eternal).

As Cronen (2001) described it, this position was challenged by Aristotle and his ideas of "practical wisdom." While supporting Platonic ideals of truth, Aristotle also developed ideas of *phronesis,* or "practical wisdom," which could be developed through *praxis,* an art rather than a science, which was concerned with exploring particulars rather than generalities and would embrace the changeability of the human world rather than adhere to the fixed world of the natural sciences. Cronen (2001) presented the idea of practical wisdom as creating "a situated ability to perform in the moment" (p. 16). This statement emphasizes the contextual and temporal aspects of praxis, that it is performed in particular contexts at particular times.

Practical theory thus differs from classical ideas about discovering eternal truths, and it also opens up possibilities for integrating theory and practice. Practice is not simply dismissed as "untrue," but, rather, is embraced as being important and needing a different kind of inquiry. The concept of a type of theory that is "good" in the way it addresses practice concerns has since been explored by a number of writers, following the statement by Lewin (1948), "Nothing is so practical as a good theory" (p. xi). As Van de Ven (1989) argued, however, "Although most of us can readily point to an example of a good theory, we are hard pressed to systematically articulate how and why a theory is good or better than an alternative theory" (p. 486).

Practical Theory Development

While the separation of theory and practice may have historical antecedents, this traditional stance has recently been challenged in ways that point to the possibility of research and practice working together. This does not just mean the development of *applied research,* as Cronen (2001) pointed out, in which the usual theories are simply introduced into practice, but a development in which theory and practice are integrated throughout. The example in Box 9.3 shows how this could happen through the use of multiple methodologies.

Box 9.3   Appreciative Organizational Theory

By Mark Edwards

Inquiring appreciatively into the conceptual diversity of organizational theory means that the positive contributions of multiple theories are acknowledged and selectively included within our explanations and meaning-making endeavors. Constructing explanations of organizational life requires an appreciative respect for those who create theoretical perspectives, just as working with organizations requires a positive regard for those who live out and coauthor organizational life. AI has its place in those dark and secret corners where theory is born, just as it does in those arenas where the practical realities of organizational life are elicited, sampled, collected, analyzed, and disseminated. Figure 9.3 is a schematic representation of the notion that AI rightfully involves both conceptual and applied phases.

Researchers don't enter into the inquiry process as blank states. They bring with them bounded assumptions and particular interpretive lenses. AI in the context of the theory development side of this cycle opens up these limited definitions, domains, and systems to a much broader, interpretive scope. In terms of the enactive side of this cycle, a more integrative theoretical vision reinforces the researcher's capacity to collect the relevant data, to adequately interpret propositions, to draw authentic inferences, and to meaningfully evaluate the success, or otherwise, of any implementations. Appreciation and integration of conceptual diversity support and inspire the appreciation and uncovering of individuals' and organizational diversity.

Multiparadigm inquiry and integral methodological pluralism are examples of AI in the realm of theory and ideas. They acknowledge that (a) all theories offer some positive contribution to our knowledge in a particular field; (b) all theories capture some positive view of the future; (c) all theories are, in a sense, dreams about human potential; and (d) all theories provide an opportunity for expanded conversations with those who take a different perspective.

So, let's be appreciative in meeting the theoretical predilections of the other as well as in meeting the lived experience of the other. Let's recognize that theory development is definitively pluralistic, yet based on a shared motive for uncovering mystery, for enriching experience, and for disclosing new visions. As David Cooperrider pointed out, "AI asks us to pay special attention to 'the best of the past and present'—in order to 'ignite the collective imagination of what might be'" (as cited in Lord, 2005). In addition to our affirming encounters with organizations and their members, I take Cooperrider's call here to refer to the value of attending to the diversity of our theoretical imaginings and to the capacity for integrative theories to ignite hopeful visions of our future.

Bibliography

Lord, J. G. (2005). *Appreciative inquiry and the quest: A new theory and methodology of human development.* Cleveland, OH: Philanthropic Quest International. Available at http://www.appreciative-inquiry.org/

e 9.3   The Cycles of AI

Appreciative Inquiry in Practice

Applied Research, Theory, & Evaluation

Providing reliable, relevant evidence and stories that support

Discovery Process
Dream Phase
Design Phase
Delivery Phase
Evaluation Phase
Lived Encounters

Conceptual Visions "Theory"

Conceptual Systems
Multiple Relationships
Diverse Domains
Multiple Definitions

Appreciative Inquiry in Theory Development

Providing meaningful, useful integrative explanatory frameworks

Theory Building

Other attempts to bring research and practice together include, as mentioned, the work on *action research*, with the aim of responding to and engendering action in a practice setting, which Gergen (2003) has described as "gaining steady momentum within the social sciences, offering a welcome and significant alternative to the typical fare of rarefied assessments of the status quo" (p. 41). A summary of action research was given in Chapter 3, but here it is useful to revisit the definition given by Kemmis and McTaggart (1998):

Action Research

> A form of collective enquiry undertaken by participants in social situations in order to improve the rationality and justice of their own social or educational practice, as well as their understanding of these practices and the situations in which these practices are carried out. (p. 5)

This definition encapsulates some of the key dimensions of action research, the collective and situated nature of inquiry and the goals of exploring practice. Action research starts with an exploration of practice and the issues, problems, and solutions that are part of the practice world. From this, plans for action or change are drawn up and implemented. This implementation is evaluated and outcomes identified, which may lead to further development or ideas for change and further evaluation—action research can be an ongoing process. As Gergen (2003) argued, however, it is important that action research does not become simply a debate about technical methods: "Ideally such endeavours should be linked with a broader vision of human functioning, one that can act as a source of continuous reflection and enrichment" (p. 41).

Key to the debates about action research are the issues of how research validity can be maintained despite what some would see as the "contamination" of engagement with the contingent world of practice. These concerns come from a focus on practice activity, and not that it is merely seen as changeable: The aim of action research is to *change practice*. If it has not done so, then the action research has not done what it set out to do. In the action research model, then, changeability (which makes some feel that practice is too fluid to fit in with ideas of "unchangeable truth") is the goal.

While action research involves a focus on action, other practice development approaches that have incorporated changeability and integrated theory and practice have done so with different foci, for example, Pearce and Cronen's "coordinated management of meaning" (CMM) (Cronen, 2001, p. 14). This approach focuses on the ways the meanings of events are collectively reinterpreted to form a basis for action. CMM is a practical theory that "offers principles informed by engagement in the details of lived experience that facilitate joining with others to produce change" (Cronen, 2001, p. 14).

Buttle (1994) summarized CMM as follows:

> A theory of human communication which synthesizes elements of philosophical pragmatism, rules theory, systems theory and later Wittgensteinian language philosophy. (p. 76)

Buttle (1994) cited Cronen, Pearce, and Tomm (1985) and their claim, in one of the first papers written on CMM, that communication is "the locus of processes through which persons co-create, manage and transform the social reality of which they are themselves a part" (p. 203). According to Buttle, when following CMM, "Rather than co-orienting to a common set of referential meanings, people interpret the actions and speech of others and co-ordinate their actions accordingly. This interpretative and co-ordinative process produces the social reality in which persons live" (pp. 76–77).

As Pearce and Pearce (2003) argued, the most basic of these processes is "the knack of looking 'at' communication, not 'through it,' to things that are thought to be more real or substantial" (p. 40). In other words, effort is directed toward exploring the way people describe their world and the way this shapes their activity, rather than simply treating communication as a straightforward report on reality. This has a link to social constructionist ideas about how the world is constructed through dialogue (see Chapter 3). The process is a complex one, however, given the diverse ideas that people have about the world. As McNamee (2003) put it, "Since we all inhabit many different relationships and communities . . . the potential for constructing very diverse and incompatible ways of being in the world is great" (p. 23).

❖ PRAGMATISM

Both action research and CMM share some core characteristics, importantly, the way in which theory and practice are brought together. Both approaches also pay a tribute to the philosophical position of *pragmatism,* a school of thought that originated in the American work of James and Dewey, which presented arguments for the need for philosophy that would address and explore the issues and concerns of practice. This has involved a rethinking of classical notions of truth as something detached from activity, but, as Rorty (1999) stated,

We cannot regard truth as a goal of inquiry. The purpose of inquiry is to achieve agreement among human beings about what to do, to bring consensus on the end to be achieved and the means to be used to achieve those ends. Inquiry that does not achieve co-ordination of behaviour is not inquiry but simply wordplay. (p. xxv)

Pragmatism, therefore, sees the goal of inquiry not as arriving at an eternal truth, but as developing ideas that help people to do things. This process of choosing what it is that we want to do, of course, entails moral choices; that is, we decide on the basis of our values about what is important or desirable. This "practical knowledge," then, is firmly embedded in the way in which we think and act in our world. Such "groundedness" is a feature of pragmatism, which in part rose in response to classical theories of eternal truth. The classical approach not only dismissed practice as menial but also created a notion of truth as being something outside or external to human experience: If the human world was so contingent and changing, then the truth must lie outside human life. A focus on external standards of truth was resisted by pragmatists, who argued that we should be exploring the dimensions of human experience rather than appealing to an unknowable and mystical "other force." Pragmatists adopted this antimetaphysical stance, with a later expression from Rorty (1989) arguing as follows:

Truth cannot be out there—cannot exist independently of the human mind—because sentences cannot so exist, or be out there. The world is out there, but descriptions of the world are not. Only descriptions of the world can be true or false. The world on its own—unaided by the describing activities of human beings—cannot. (p. 5)

The emphasis on human endeavor and action developed by pragmatists led to a concern with the ways in which people perceived and described their world, as these ideas shaped their actions. Rorty (1989) articulated this interest in language and description as a project of "redescription"; that is, we need to redescribe the way we see the world and also the way we can know about the way we see the world. According to Rorty (1989), our actions are not something that we can "find out about" using traditional models of science and truth, but, rather, something we need to engage in and understand as a community of people rather than detached observers, with awareness of human goals and values.

Pragmatism has obvious connections to some of the "worldviews" outlined in this book. An example is the discussion in Chapter 3 about *social constructionism*. The idea that we co-construct our social worlds through our conversations and interactions is expressed in McNamee's (2003) account of working with school staff to co-construct positive futures:

> Briefly, constructionism focuses our attention on the social processes by which people create and maintain realities. This entails focusing on what people do together. Consequently, constructionists focus attention on language practices (all embodied activities of persons relating together). (p. 23)

This takes us to the particular case of AI. McNamee has said that she regards AI as "a useful elaboration of social construction," and the links she makes have to do with the shared interests of social constructionism and AI in the way that conversations are generative; that is, they both involve participants in the process of storying the world. AI particularly focuses on positive stories, or, as McNamee stated, "If what we do together creates the possibilities and constraints within which we live, then how might our realities change if we replace deficit-based language, which focuses on what is not working, with talk of what is working?" (p. 24).

At this point, a brief summary of how the discussion of AI in this chapter has led to this point may be helpful. By returning to philosophical positions about truth and how it can be explored, pragmatism was brought into play, that is, the idea that theory can be evaluated in terms of its practice validity rather than any abstract criteria. This took the discussion in two directions. First, it introduced an alternative way of thinking about research and inquiry that places debates about validity and bias in a different light. To develop ideas that are useful for practice, an approach is required that is engaged with practice actions and contexts, one that supports inclusivity and selectivity as being appropriate to our task, rather than an obstacle to investigation. This, in turn, also places many of the topics covered in Chapters 5 and 6, such as planning and carrying out AI studies, in a different light. Throughout those chapters, the demands of planning and carrying out an AI study were contrasted with traditional approaches. In Chapter 5, for example, the AI drive toward considering communities of inquiry was juxtaposed with the idea of research being carefully mapped out by individuals or clearly defined teams. The traditional criteria can make AI studies seem chaotic. Similarly, when it involves collaborative action, the AI process of data collection can seem incongruent with orthodox ideas of researcher consistency and competence.

The second avenue of discussion led to a consideration of the development of theory, suggesting that it may need to be judged primarily by the way it can contribute to practice. Again, this may entail engagement with the world of practice, in order to understand the key questions or issues and consider useful outcomes. These points were explored in most detail in Chapters 7 and 8, which examine analysis and communication. The notion of collaborative data analysis, in which data are explored by a range of participants, moves away from ideas of predetermined analysis, in which data are collected and then analyzed with defined objectives in mind, toward a process that is more flexible and responsive to the developing and changing interests of participants. The communication of research in AI, as described in Chapter 8, is similarly responsive and inclusive, with messages tailored to the interests of different audiences.

Constructions of AI research are very different from traditional ideas—their processes are different and so are their goals. In this book, for the most part, the discussion of AI has been put forth in a positive light. It is important, however, to recognize and reflect on other views of AI that are more cautionary. Engaging with these alternative positions is, indeed, congruent with AI, as Goldberg (2001) argued:

> Not only is an appreciative frame of reference crucial to appreciative inquiry, but so too is inquiry. Inquiry is a key element of "dialogue" . . . a process in which individuals explore with each other their "ways of thinking," their assumptions and mind-sets, in order to arrive at deep levels of understanding. . . . Inquiry is about asking questions from a standpoint of genuine curiosity (rather than asking questions to make one's own point, as is frequently the case); being willing to delve behind surface conclusions by exploring how those conclusions were arrived at, examining one's own and others' assumptions out loud; and being open to revising one's thinking based on new information. (pp. 56–57)

The following section issues some cautionary comments. While this may seem paradoxically unappreciative, these points are made in the spirit of balancing out the debate and directing the reader to the important nature of critical reflection, which allows people to engage with different perspectives rather than deny or dismiss them. The cautionary comments are offered here in the spirit of broadening the discussion and raising awareness that AI, if adopted without reflection, is not an automatic answer to all questions and that caveats and qualifications need to be considered. This leads to some ideas about how AI might develop as a research methodology and what might need to change for this to happen.

❖ CAUTIONARY COMMENTS

The preceding discussion has pointed to a new way of developing AI as a research approach, but this is not to say that it represents an unequivocal approval of AI and that full and uncritical acceptance is the only way forward. There are many important cautionary points to consider.

First, echoing previously identified comments about the problem of focusing on the positive at the expense of the negative or neutral is the point that constructing every description as appreciative is not necessarily useful for practice. The following quotation is taken from comments made by a nurse during an action research study (Sharp, 2005), in which she reported on the positive feedback given to a colleague:

> She said . . . "I know I'm a good A & E nurse because my colleagues tell me I'm a good A & E nurse—and the doctors tell me that I'm a good nurse. I'm well known. I can get a drunk out of here in 20 minutes. I just pull him off the trolley by his ear and take him out the door." She was valued because she cleared the spaces. But it ain't good practice! (p. 16)

Although this comment arose during an action research study rather than an AI study, the story it tells seems very appreciative. At the same time, however, it is difficult to imagine how this would amount to anything more than a reinforcement of a rather brusque approach to managing drunks. Of course the judgment that the response was brusque is based on a set of values that promote the respectful treatment of people as individuals rather than obstacles. Similarly, the feedback from an AI study may do nothing to promote reflection without reference to the principles and values that shape practice. As Rogers and Fraser 2003 stated, "Appreciation is not just looking at the good stuff" (p. 75). The nurse's story could, on the other hand, be appreciated as an efficient response to disruptive or time-consuming patients and the needs of colleagues, but the discussion may need to go on to explore ways in which this positive assessment could be built on to promote efficiency in ways more in tune with values and goals.

Another response to positive stories is to do nothing. The example in Box 9.4 tells a story of an AI study that involved a lot of energy and planning and was seen as constructive by participants (this story was told in Chapter 6, but it is worth revisiting here to reflect on the message it has for using research). The study did not have the impact that it could have had, however, because of the response of the people with the power to make changes.

Box 9.4   Reflections on Using AI in School Development

By Maha Shuayb

Several elements of the AI were used in my research titled "Towards a Theory of Care: An Explorative Study of Students', Teachers', and Principals' Views in Secondary Schools in Lebanon." The research incorporated elements of AI. Two questionnaires that included positive, open-ended questions were designed to explore students' and teachers' views in 14 schools. Appreciative-focus group workshops with students were also conducted with 120 students. At the end of the research, students were given an evaluation form.

The evaluation form revealed that the majority of students believed that positive questioning helped them to focus on what works in their schools. It also allowed them to feel more connected with what goes on in their schools. Some students felt that this experience encouraged them think of solutions to issues in their schools, rather than complaining. They also felt more relaxed in answering these questions because they were not criticizing anyone. Nonetheless, some students pointed out that it is important to highlight the negative experiences in order to understand the complete situation at a school.

The use of AI techniques enabled me to identify the best practices in the schools. Positive questions helped me to gain access to the schools, which was especially important because most of the teachers and school principals in Lebanon were not familiar with the idea of research. Thus, using AI, which looks into what works in the school, instead of the negatives, facilitates the research process. AI was also effective in the construction of developmental plans for the schools. However, the school principals refused to take the plan seriously that was designed by the students, as well as the recommendations made by teachers. Hence, while AI as a theory underpinning developmental research facilitated the research procedures and planning development, it failed in bringing about change and progress in the schools.

Shuayb's account points to a dimension of AI work that can limit its impact, and that is *power*. This has been discussed elsewhere in this book, particularly in Chapter 4, but here it is timely to reiterate the point that we cannot be naive about issues of power. If an AI study produces findings or ideas that do not accord with the ideas of the people with the resources and power to make things happen, it is difficult to see how these findings can be acted on. There is, however, a discussion to be had of what is meant by *power* here. Gergen (2003) and others in the social constructionist school of thought have pointed to the way that power can be cocreated through language: If we *talk* about people as having power, then they will have it, as we respond obediently (or resentfully) to their wishes. Gergen has also pointed to Foucault and his work on the construction of identities of power and powerlessness through discursive practices (Foucault, 1978).

This set of ideas opens up some possibilities for responding to discourses about power and control, namely, that these discourses can be examined critically to determine how they arise and are maintained and what options may exist for changing the ways in which we might respond. These options, however, run some risk of dismissing issues of power as being "just talk." From this, it might be argued that power is not "real" and can be ignored. This does not acknowledge the pervasiveness and strength of perceptions of power or the difficulties faced by anyone trying to challenge them. As Rogers and Fraser (2003) argued,

> We are also concerned about the overemphasis on how perceptions affect reality without due concern for how reality can intrude on people's lives. There are many aspects of lived reality that are not invented and exist despite our mental state; grinding poverty, gender inequality, violence, and disease are some examples. (p. 77)

In short, while the notion of power as being co-constructed may offer some opportunities for change, it cannot dismiss all aspects of life as it is lived by many. AI needs to take care that it is inclusive of power differentials while exploring possibilities for change.

Following on from Rogers and Fraser's (2003) identification of aspects of lived reality is their general concern about the optimism on which AI is founded: "Appreciative Inquiry is based on a seductively plausible causal model: that by highlighting the positive, we can help bring about the positive outcomes we describe" (p. 76). They challenged this assumption, citing Norem's (2001) work on "defensive pessimism" as an approach that many people find useful and appropriate, given the way they feel about their situations.

❖ CONCLUSION

This chapter started by outlining the temptations that this book could fall into, the temptation to engage in a competitive debate about the "best" framework for research or to present a set of definitive conclusions about the way AI should develop. These temptations were critiqued, but not necessarily avoided. While the concept of negative capability was affirmed, it was not necessarily followed—the conventions of writing did push toward a resounding conclusion about the way things should be.

To redeem this situation, albeit in a limited way, one can argue that AI as a research approach seems to be at a formative stage in development. While the OD strand of AI has had much attention, AI research has had less, and this can be attributed to the long-standing frameworks against which AI research has been assessed. These traditional frameworks are part of the established structure of research support, and AI needs to respond creatively and responsively. AI can be research for change, drawing on OD traditions, but this change may require a different way of doing research and a different way of evaluating it. Developing these different ways may take a sustained effort from AI researchers.

A sustained effort might be compromised by a superficial use of AI. Bushe (2000), for example, pointed to the way that AI is a term that is used indiscriminately:

> I am concerned that as appreciative inquiry becomes "fashionable" two undesirable things are happening. One is that any inquiry that focuses on the "positive" in some way gets called appreciative inquiry (AI). . . . A second concern is that some practitioners . . . can develop a zealous attention to "appreciation" without any theoretical rhyme or reason to their practice. Promoting appreciation where there has been little can, of itself, generate a wave of energy and enthusiasm but that will go away just as quickly as the next challenge or tragedy to a social system rears its head. (p. 99)

Bushe's comments point to the need for careful and considered reflection on AI to avoid the dangers of empty slogans without reflection and thought.

As a conclusion, then, this chapter falls short of a clear way forward, and although there is a general call to do more AI research and to work these issues out, this is not precisely prescribed. Perhaps the most appropriate thought that arises here is the phrase that Rorty has used when talking about the way forward for practical theory. Reason (2003) reported a conversation with Rorty, when talking about the project of redescription, who said,

> What I was dubious about . . . was, do [people] really need a new kind of language or do they just need less talk about what it is they are doing or what our method is? It's as if you are giving them a new meta-discourse instead of just saying skip the meta-discourse and just get on with it. (Rorty, as cited in Reason, 2003, p. 109)

This book, then, follows Rorty in suggesting that perhaps we can develop AI only if we "just get on with it."

❖ EXERCISE 1: REFLECTING ON THE DISTINCTIVENESS OF AI

Think about an example of a study relevant to your area of practice. Think about the language used and what this may convey about the relationship between the researchers and the people being researched. Does this study reflect the idea that an organization is a problem to be solved?

If you were to develop an AI study on the basis that an organization is a miracle to be embraced, how would your study be different? You might like to think about the following points:

- Who might participate in the study?
- What questions might be asked?
- How could stories be generated?
- How might sense be made of stories?
- How might they be told to others?

❖ EXERCISE 2: MAPPING THE POSITION OF AI

Represent the characteristics of AI and its differences from and similarities to other approaches in a visual way, using the dimensions of participation. This could be artwork, for example, a sculpture or picture that draws out and reflects key principles of AI. Inclusivity might be conveyed through images of embraces and arms reaching out. You could also use diagrams and flowcharts to represent AI processes or connections.

References

Altheide, D., & Johnson, J. (1994). Criteria for assessing interpretive validity in qualitative research. In N. Denzin & Y. Lincoln (Eds.), *Handbook of qualitative research* (pp. 485–499). Thousand Oaks, CA: Sage.

Amir, H. (2005). Globalization and knowledge hierarchy through the eyes of a quiz show. *European Journal of Social Policy, 18*(4), 385–405.

Anderson, H. (1999). Collaborative learning communities. In S. McNamee & K. J. Gergen (Eds.), *Relational responsibility: Resources for sustainable dialogue* (pp. 65–70). Thousand Oaks, CA: Sage.

Atkinson, P., Coffey, A., Delamont, S., Lofland, J., & Lofland, L. (Eds.). (2001). *Handbook of ethnography.* London: Sage.

Bobasi, S., Jackson, D., & Wilkes, L. (2005). Fieldwork in nursing research: Positionality, practicalities, and predicaments. *Journal of Advanced Nursing, 51*(5), 493–501.

Burnes, B. (2004.). Kurt Lewin and complexity theories: Back to the future? *Journal of Change Management, 4*(4), 309–325.

Burr, V. (1995). *An introduction to social constructionism.* London: Routledge.

Bushe, G. R. (1995). Advances in appreciative inquiry as an organization development intervention. *Organization Development Journal, 13*(3), 14–22.

Bushe, G. R. (2000). Five theories of change embedded in appreciative inquiry. In D. L. Cooperrider, P. Sorenson, D. Whitney, & T. Yeager (Eds.), *Appreciative inquiry: An emerging direction for organization development* (pp. 99–110). Champaign, IL: Stipes.

Buttle, F. A. (1994). The co-ordinated management of meaning: A case exemplar of a new consumer research technology. *European Journal of Marketing, 28*(8/9), 76–99.

Clandinin, D. J., & Huber, J. (2002). Narrative inquiry: Toward understanding life's artistry. *Curriculum Inquiry, 32*(2), 161–169.

Coffey, A. (1999). *The ethnographic self.* London: Sage.

Coghlan, A. T., Preskill, H., & Catsambas, T. T. (2003). An overview of appreciative inquiry in evaluation. *New Directions for Evaluation, 100*, 5–22.

Conle, C. (1999). Why narrative? Which narrative? Struggling with time and place in life and research. *Curriculum Inquiry, 29*(1), 7–32.

Cooperrider, D. (1986). *Appreciative inquiry: Toward a methodology for understanding and enhancing organizational innovation.* Doctoral dissertation, Western Reserve University, Cleveland, OH.

Cooperrider, D., & Whitney, D. (1999). When stories have wings: How relational responsibility opens possibilities for action. In S. McNamee & K. J. Gergen (Eds.), *Relational responsibility: Resources for sustainable dialogue.* (pp. 57–64). Thousand Oaks, CA: Sage.

Cooperrider, D. L., Whitney, D., & Stavros, J. M. (2003). *The appreciative inquiry handbook.* Bedford, OH: Lakeshore Communications.

Cronen, V. E. (2001). Practical theory, practical art, and the pragmatic-systemic account of inquiry. *Communication Theory, 11*(1), 14–35.

Cronen, V. E., Pearce, W. B., & Tomm, K. (1985). A dialectical view of social change. In K. J. Gergen & K. E. Davis (Eds.), The social construction of the person (pp. 203–224). New York: Springer-Verlag.

de Laine, M. (2001). *Fieldwork, participation, and practice: Ethics and dilemmas of qualitative research.* London: Sage.

Delbecq, A. (1975). *Group techniques for programme planning.* Glenview, IL: Scott, Foresman.

Delbecq, A. L., & Van de Ven, A. H. (1971). A group process model for problem identification and program planning. *Journal of Applied Behavioral Science, 7,* 466–492.

Denzin, N., & Lincoln, Y. (Eds.). (1998). *Collecting and interpreting qualitative materials.* Thousand Oaks, CA: Sage.

Descartes, R. (1641/1960). *Metaphysical meditations.* Harmondsworth, England: Penguin Books.

Dewey, J. (1960). *The quest for certainty.* New York: Capricorn Books. (Original work published 1929)

Egg, P., Schratz-Hadwich, B., Trübswasse, G., & Walker, R. (2004). *Seeing beyond violence: Children as researchers. Children in Colombia, India, Nicaragua, and Thailand.* Innsbruck, Austria: Hermann Gmeiner Akademie.

Eisner, E., & Powell, K. (2002). Art in science? *Curriculum Inquiry 32*(2), 131–159.

Elbaz-Luwisch, F. (2002). Writing as inquiry: Storying the teaching self in writing workshops. *Curriculum Inquiry, 32*(4), 403–428.

Fontana, J. S. (2004). A methodology for critical science in nursing. *Advances in Nursing Science, 27*(2), 93–101.

Foucault, M. (1978). *The history of sexuality* (Vol. 1., R. Hurley, Trans.). New York: Pantheon.

Freire, P. (1999). *Pedagogy of the oppressed.* New York: Continuum.

Gergen, K. (1982). *Toward transformation in social knowledge.* New York: Springer-Verlag.

Gergen, K. J. (1999). *An invitation to social construction.* Thousand Oaks, CA: Sage.

Gergen, K. J. (2003). Action research and orders of democracy. *Action Research, 1*(1), 39–56.

Glaser, B., & Strauss, A. (1967). *The discovery of grounded theory.* Chicago: Aldine.

Goldberg, R. A. (2001). Implementing a professional development system through appreciative inquiry. *Leadership & Organization Development Journal, 22*(2), 56–61.

Gubrium, J., & Holstein, J. (1999). At the border of narrative and ethnography. *Journal of Contemporary Ethnography, 28*(5), 561–573.

Hamel, G. (2000). *Leading the revolution.* Boston: Harvard Business School Press.

Hammond, S. (1996). *The thin book of appreciative inquiry.* Plano, TX: Thin Book Publishing.

Hertz, R. (1996). Introduction: Ethics, reflexivity, and voice. *Qualitative Sociology, 19*(1), 3–9.

Holliday, A. (2002). *Doing and writing qualitative research.* London: Sage.

Holloway, I. (1997). *Basic concepts for qualitative research.* London: Blackwell Science.

Horner, M. (1997). Leadership theory: Past, present and future. *Total Performance Management, 3*(4), 270–287.

Johnson, G., & Leavitt, W. (2001). Building on success: Transforming organizations through an appreciative inquiry. *Public Personnel Management, 30*(1), 129–136.

Jorgensen, D. L. (1989). *Participant observation: A methodology for human studies.* Newbury Park, CA: Sage.

Kemmis, S., & McTaggart, R. (Eds.). (1998). *The action research planner* (3rd ed.). Victoria, Australia: Deakin University Press.

Knippen, J. T., & Green, B. T. (1997). Problem solving. *Journal of Workplace Learning, 9*(3), 98–99.

Kuhn, T. S. (1970). *The structure of scientific revolutions.* Chicago: University of Chicago Press.

Labov, W. (1972). *Language in the inner city: Studies in the Black English vernacular.* Philadelphia: University of Pennsylvania Press.

Lewin, G. (Ed.). (1948). *Resolving social conflicts: Selected papers on group dynamics by Kurt Lewin.* New York: Harper & Brothers.

Lewin, K. (1945). The Research Center for Group Dynamics at Massachusetts Institute of Technology. *Sociometry, 8*(2), 126–135.

Marx, K. (1858/1973). *Grundrisse: Foundations of the critique of political economy.* Harmondsworth, UK: Penguin Books.

Mayo, E. (1933). *The human problem of an industrial civilisation.* New York: Macmillan.

McNamee, S. (2003). Appreciative evaluation within a conflicted educational context. *New Directions for Evaluation, 100,* 23–40.

McNamee, S., & Gergen, K. J. (1999). *Relational responsibility: Resources for sustainable dialogue.* London: Sage.

Michael, S. (2005). The promise of appreciative inquiry as an interview tool for field research. *Development in Practice, 15*(2), 222–230.

Midgley, M. (1989). *Wisdom, information, and wonder: What is knowledge for?* London: Routledge and Kegan Paul.

Midgley, M. (1992). *Science as salvation: A modern myth and its meaning.* London: Routledge and Kegan Paul.

Morgan, G. (1997). *Images of organization* (2nd ed.). London: Sage.

Nelson, L. (2003). A case study in organisational change: Implications for theory. *Learning Organization, 10*(1), 18–30.

Norem, J. (2001). *The positive power of negative thinking: Using defensive pessimism to harness anxiety and perform at your peak.* New York: Basic Books.

Nussbaum, M. (2002). Patriotism and cosmopolitanism. In J. Cohen (Ed.), *For love of country: Debating the limits of patriotism* (pp. 2–29). Boston: Beacon Press.

Patton, M. Q. (2003). Inquiry into appreciative evaluation. *New Directions for Evaluation, 100,* 85–98.

Pearce, W. B, & Pearce, K. A. (2003). Taking a communication perspective on dialogue. In R. Anderson, L. A. Baxter, & K. N. Cissna (Eds.), *Dialogue: Theorizing difference in communication studies* (pp. 39–56). Thousand Oaks, CA: Sage.

Plsek, P. E. P., & Wilson, T. (2001). Complexity, leadership and management in healthcare organisations. *British Medical Journal, 323*(7315), 746–749.

Popper, K. (1963). *Conjectures and refutations.* London: Routledge and Kegan Paul.

Reason, P. (1994). *Participation in human inquiry.* London: Sage.

Reason, P. (2003). Pragmatist philosophy and action research: Readings and conversation with Richard Rorty. *Action Research 1*(1), 103–123.

Reason, P., & Bradbury, H. (2001). Inquiry and participation in search of a world worthy of human aspiration. In P. Reason & H. Bradbury (Eds.), *Handbook of action research: Participative inquiry and practice* (pp. 1–14). London: Sage.

Reason, P., & Torbert, W. (2001). The action turn: Toward a transformational social science. *Concepts and Transformation, 6*(1), 1–37.

Reed, J., Pearson, P., Douglas, B., Swinburne, S., & Wilding, H. (2002). Going home from hospital: An appreciative inquiry study. *Health and Social Care and the Community, 10*(1), 36–45.

Reed J., & Procter, S. (Eds.). (1994). *Practitioner research in health care.* London: Chapman Hall.

Reed, J., Stanley, D., & Clarke, C. (2004). *Health, well-being, and older people.* Bristol, UK: Policy Press.

Reid, N. G., & Boore, J. R. P. (1987). *Research methods and statistics in health care.* London: Edwards Arnold.

Reinharz, S. (1979). *On becoming a social scientist: From survey research and participant observation to experiential analysis.* San Francisco: Jossey-Bass.

Rogers, P. J., & Fraser, D. (2003). Appreciating appreciative inquiry. *New Directions for Evaluation, 100,* 75–83.

Rorty, R. (1989). *Contingency, irony, and solidarity.* Cambridge, MA: Cambridge University Press.

Rorty, R. (1999). *Philosophy and social hope.* London: Penguin.

Savin-Baden, M. (2004). Achieving reflexivity: Moving researchers from analysis to interpretation in collaborative inquiry *Journal of Social Work Practice, 18*(3), 365–378.

Schön, D. A. (1983). *The reflective practitioner.* New York: Basic Books.

Schön, D. A. (1987). *Educating the reflective practitioner.* San Francisco: Jossey-Bass.

Schratz, M., & Walker, R. (1995). *Research as social change: New opportunities for qualitative research.* London: Routledge.

Sharp, C. (2005). *The improvement of public sector delivery: supporting evidence based practice through action research.* Edinburg, Scotland: Scottish Executive Social Research.

Shotter, J. (2006). Understanding process from within: An argument for "with-ness" thinking. *Organization Studies, 27*(4), 585–604.

Silverman, D. (1985). *Qualitative methodology and sociology.* London: Gower.

Staff of Mountbatten Ward, Wright, M., & Baker, A. (2005). The effects of appreciative inquiry interviews on staff in the U.K. National Health Service. *International Journal of Health Care Quality Assurance, 18*(1), 41–61.

Steier, F. (Ed.). (1991). *Research and reflexivity.* London: Sage.

Stevenson, C. (1995). Reflections on evaluating a course of family therapy. In J. Reed & S. Procter (Eds.), *Practitioner research in health care: The inside story* (pp. 99–112). London: Chapman & Hall.

Stevenson, C. (2005). Practical inquiry/theory in nursing. *Journal of Advanced Nursing, 50*(2), 196–203.

Tomm, K. (1999). Co-constructing responsibility. In S. McNamee & K. J. Gergen (Eds.), *Relational responsibility: Resources for sustainable dialogue* (pp. 129–138). Thousand Oaks, CA: Sage.

Van de Ven, A. H. (1989). Nothing is quite so practical as a good theory. *Academy of Management Review, 14*(4), 486–489.

Van Maanen, J. (Ed.). (1995). *Representation in ethnography.* Thousand Oaks, CA: Sage.

Wang, C. C., & Redwood-Jones, Y. A. (2001). Photovoice ethics: Perspectives from Flint Photovoice. *Health Education & Behaviour, 28*(5), 560–572.

Watkins, J. M., & Mohr, B. J. (2001). *Appreciative inquiry: Change at the speed of imagination.* San Francisco: Jossey-Bass.

Whitney, D. (1998). Let's change the subject and change our organization: An appreciative inquiry approach to organization change. *Career Development International, 3,* 314–319.

Wiles, J. L., Rosenberg, M. W., & Kearns, R. A. (2005). Narrative analysis as a strategy for understanding interview talk in geographic research. *Area 37*(1), 89–99.

Willis, P. (2000). *The ethnographic imagination.* Oxford: Policy Press.

Wittgenstein, L. (1967). *Philosophical investigations.* London: Blackwell.

Yin, R. K. (1984). *Case study research: Design and methods.* London: Sage.

Zeldin, T. (1998). *Conversations.* London: Harvill Press.

Index

About the Author

Jan Reed is Professor of Health Care for Older People at the University of Northumbria at Newcastle, in the United Kingdom, teaching and supervising postgraduate students in research methods, particularly qualitative research. She has authored or coauthored a number of books and reports, including *Nurse Education: A Reflective Approach* (1993), which drew on the work of Donald Schön, and *Practitioner Research in Health Care* (1994), which explored issues of research carried out by practitioners on their practice. She has also coauthored *Philosophy and Nursing* (1996); *Opening Up Care: Enabling Practice in Institutions* (1999); and *Health, Well-Being, and Older People* (2004). She has also authored or coauthored a number of research reports, including "Growing Old Is Not for Cowards" (2003).

She came across Appreciative Inquiry when working with older people and community workers exploring "going home from hospital," and, since then, she has developed ideas of Appreciative Inquiry and also of collaborative research with older people, carrying out projects, writing papers, and establishing an informal Older People's Research Group (OPRG). She was a member of the European-Union-funded thematic network "CARMEN," which explored services for older people across Europe and evaluated the network using Appreciative inquiry. She is currently coeditor of the *International Journal of Older People Nursing* and is a member of the Centre for Collaborative Gerontology at Northumbria University. She is convener of the "Years Ahead" working group on research and older people. Current interests include life in care homes for older people and international perspectives on growing older.

About the Contributors

Julie Barnes
University of London

Bernie Carter
University of Central Lancashire

Jeanie Cockell
Jeanie Cockell Consulting, Inc.

Glenda Anne Cook
Northumbria University

Mark Edwards
University of Western Australia

Mary Emery
North Central Center for Rural Development

Audrey Lax
Older People's Research Group at Northumbria University

Tim Luckcock
Liverpool Hope University

Elsie Richardson
Older People's Research Group at Northumbria University

Marie-Claire Richer
McGill University

Charly Ryan
University of Winchester

Maha Shuayb
University of Cambridge